THREE DECADES OF
THE DERBY

A Collection of Stories from Thirty Years
of Participation in Martha's Vineyard
Fall Fishing Classic

RON DOMURAT

ISBN: 0692203249
ISBN 13: 9780692203248

Photo Credits
Cover photo by the author

Photos pages 4, 17, 33, 61 courtesy Mark Carlson
Photo page 49, Charlie Barr
Photo page 95, Roger Ardanowski
Photo page 121 Pete Gardow
All other photos by the author

Back cover photo by Ron Domurat Jr.

Cover Design by CreateSpace

DEDICATION

This book is dedicated to my ol' Martha's Vineyard friends and fishing partners, Don Mohr, Abe Williams, Gordon Ditchfield, Al Angelone, Marsh Bryan and Walter Lison. I want to keep their memories alive somehow. *RIP Don, Abe, Gordon and Ang!*

Also, to my brother Bob who introduced me to the sport of surfcasting, and my good friend Jack McIlduff who introduced me to Martha's Vineyard. I will be forever grateful to these guys as they changed my life. *RIP Bob and Jack!*

And of course to my wife Barbara, she's never once complained about my other passion.

TABLE OF CONTENTS

PREFACE

For the last thirty years, the Martha's Vineyard Striped Bass and Bluefish Derby has been a big part of my life and in some respects, it's a microcosm of the rest of the time I've lived on this planet.

As in life, the Derby has its ups and downs. It can be fun and exciting, but also frustrating and disappointing. It can be happy and it can be sad. It can be exhilarating and at times, it can be boring. It even has its scary moments.

During three decades of fishing the Derby, I've been fortunate to be able to spend thousands of hours at the edge of the surf. I've had good days and bad and I've caught a lot of fish. I've seen nature at its best and at its worse. I've met people from all walks of life, most good, a few not so good, and some that I came to know well and count as close friends.

This book is about some of the Derby experiences that I've had and the people I've known, a few who now fish in a better place. It's important to me that these memories are preserved, not only for my family, but the families of those I've written about.

INTRODUCTION

For as long as I can remember I've been a fisherman. My dad taught me how to fish at a very young age and I got hooked on it. One of my oldest memories is being in a rowboat with him on Lake Hayward in Colchester, CT and hooking a small sunfish that I was afraid to touch. I remember pleading with him to take it off the hook but he wouldn't hear of it. A few years later while vacationing at the same lake, I was standing on a dock and saw a pickerel chasing sunfish in shallow water. The next day I caught a small 'sunny' and threw it back out. It got hit so hard by a big pickerel, it put a permanent set in the old bamboo casting rod.

My cousin George Jedd was a D-Day survivor and mentored me as a trout fisherman. One year, I was sick in bed the day of the local kids derby. A couple of days later he took me to the same pond and in a pouring rain storm we limited out on trout.

My uncle Frank Domurat was a barber by trade and a freshwater fishing fanatic. He was a man well ahead of his time and would buy or trap fingerling largemouth bass and keep them in an aquarium in his barber shop so he could observe their feeding habits. At one time, he held the Connecticut state record for Large and Smallmouth bass, and Northern Pike. He still holds the state record for a 12.14 lb. largemouth bass he caught in 1961 and with fishing pressure the way it is today, that record may never be broken.

I grew up in New Britain, CT and was within walking distance of four ponds that were just over the town line in Berlin. For years the ponds had been excavated by local brick makers who extracted clay that was used in brick production. The bricks were used to construct buildings all over the country. One of the companies was Stiles Brickyard and I once found one of their bricks in the rubble below the Cape Poge lighthouse.

The ponds were very deep and held good numbers of bullheads, largemouth bass and bluegills that were so big they wouldn't fit into a good size frying pan. There were also eels about as big around as a thirteen year olds wrist. Late one afternoon a friend and I threaded a night crawler onto a hook and tossed it into Merwin's Pond. We then cut the line, tied it to a small tree and left it there for the night. When we came back the next morning I retrieved the line hand over hand and hauled in a huge eel that had to weigh at least ten pounds. Once we got it on the shore we freaked out and were afraid to touch the thing, so we cut the line and watched as the beast slithered its way back to freedom. Had we thought about things like that back then, I'm sure it would have set the state record.

It was a short bike ride to the railroad tracks and then a short walk to most of the ponds and my friends and I spent many a summer day fishing and just hanging out at Merwin's, Stiles, Carbos, or the Island Pond. When it got too hot to fish, we stripped off our clothes and 'bare-assed' along the railroad tracks at Stiles, which was less than a half mile from the Berlin railroad station. On more than one occasion we got in trouble with the Berlin police after 'mooning' passing trains as they slowed to stop at the station.

I didn't get into surfcasting until the early seventies when my career as a salesman of printed continuous form computer paper took me to Long Island for a couple of years. I was running on the beach in Huntington early one morning and ran into a couple of local life-guards walking off with two good size stripers that they had caught just a few hundred yards away. I had never caught a striper in my life and was excited about the fact that stripers that big could be caught in relatively shallow water just a short cast from the beach. A few days later I walked into a local tackle shop for some advice and left with a Crack 200 reel (that I still have) along with an eight foot fiberglass rod, line, leaders, and a half dozen lures. That weekend I caught my first striper on a 5"'yellow bomber type lure.

My assignment on Long Island only lasted a couple of years but long enough for me to really get surfcasting into my blood and by the time I was transferred back to the Hartford area I knew I had to find a way to stay with it.

My brother, who was older than me by six years, had already been fishing the surf since the late sixties. Bob was a municipal firefighter and fished the southern Rhode Island surf and later the outer Cape beaches, particularly Truro and Provincetown. He owned a truck camper that he stored in Provincetown and his four days on, three days off schedule afforded him the luxury of leaving work after a four day stint, load his family and supplies in his pickup, and make the five hour trip from his home in New Britain to Provincetown. Then he would re-load the family into the camper and use a Ford Bronco as a chase vehicle to run the beaches hunting for striped bass at night, and bluefish during the day. Occasionally in the fall when his kids were back in school he would invite me to join him and I even managed to catch my one and only forty pound striper, which at the time, I was not too impressed with because it was the beginning of the last striper crash and a time when there were a lot of big fish around. A forty pound fish back then did not hold the significance it does today, and along with a number of other fish in the mid to high thirties we caught that night, the fish went right into the cooler to be sold at market the next day. I don't even have a picture of it.

I was envious of his life style but my kids were younger, and my career choice different, so I never took the plunge and went the truck camper route. I did buy an off-road vehicle (ORV) and would purchase an annual permit for Rhode Island beaches and in the fall, run those beaches looking for bluefish and stripers. But surf casting had to be fairly low on my list of priorities behind my career and later, my teenaged kids' activities, which included travelling all over New England watching them participate in their high school sport which was rowing. I later learned to row myself and got heavily involved in crew racing so most of my time from May through late October was spent on the Farmington River in Simsbury, CT practicing or travelling to races throughout the east. But once the crew season ended the lure of the surf would draw me back to the Rhode Island coast, even though it was more than a two hour drive from my home in Simsbury.

Most of my efforts at the time took place between dawn and dusk and since striper stocks were in the midst of their crash and rapidly becoming scarce, they were directed primarily toward bluefish and I spent much of my time dunking bait in front of the 'Pink House' or running the beaches from Watch Hill to Charleston looking for breaking fish. I always caught my share including some very big bluefish and a few mid size stripers, but in comparison to my brother and his friends who supported their passion by selling stripers, I never thought of myself as a good fisherman, certainly not anywhere close to being in the same league as them.

When continuous feed computer paper became a dinosaur in the early nineties and my sales career ground to a halt I found myself with more time on my hands and started to fish the Rhode Island beaches on a more regular basis. I also became a student of the game and tried to learn as much as possible about the sport. I read all I could and attended seminars at fishing shows and Rivers End Tackle in Old Saybrook, CT. I learned about places along the CT shore and by that time I had already been visiting the Vineyard for more than ten years and was able to explore new spots there as well. I even attempted to find a way into the tackle business but the economy was bad and the industry consolidating so the best I could do was find a part time job at Rivers End. But that job led to a new opportunity and prior to moving permanently to the Vineyard in 2002, I spent three years as Executive Director of the Connecticut Chapter of the Coastal Conservation Association, a fisheries advocacy group based in Houston, TX. Those three years turned out to be one of the most productive and rewarding periods of my life.

During that time I also put a couple of ideas together and developed the Hammer fishing lure and started the Dory Lure Company. The lure was simply a hexagonal piece of chrome plated brass, biased cut at both ends and dressed with a green and white fly. We were living in an apartment at the time and had no manufacturing facility so to produce the lure I would buy 8' long pieces of brass, ship them to a tool and die shop where they would be cut to size and then tumbled to remove any burrs. My brother would drill both ends for the hook and split ring and when that was completed I would deliver them to a plating facility to have the chrome finish applied. Throughout the entire process I would be at home tying the epoxy flies, one year, more than 8,000 of them. I did all the assembly work and Barbara and I would package and ship them. I later sold the business to Peter Johnson and the Roberts Lure Company. Peter still produces the lure and it's a proven favorite for catching false albacore and bonito.

THE EARLY YEARS

MY FIRST FISHING adventure to the Vineyard took place in 1981, after my friend Jack McIlduff built a home here and suggested I use it after the rental season in late September. It was not my first trip to the island because my family and I had cruised to and around the island in 1980 in a 27' Sea Ray and we spent time exploring the island via sightseeing bus. I liked the feel of the place. I did no fishing but during that trip I was amazed by the rugged rocky coast on the north shore and the twenty six miles of open beach on the south side. It all looked fishy to me so when my friend offered me the use of his house I jumped at the offer. This time however, I brought my surf rods which consisted of an 11' white Lamiglas stick that was about the size of a pool cue and an 8' two-piece honeycomb fiberglass stick. My brother had custom wrapped them for me and both were equipped with Penn 704 reels and strung with 20 lb. Ande monofilament. I still have both rods. My lure arsenal consisted primarily of 2 oz. Atom poppers and A-40 swimmers, and 2 oz. Kastmasters and Hopkins.

I didn't have much guidance but had heard about the wild bluefish action at Wasque Point at the southeastern tip of Chappaquiddick. Wasque is the southernmost point along the route of the dropping tide in Nantucket Sound which drains in a southerly direction between the fifteen miles that separate Nantucket and the Vineyard. It's like being squeezed through an hour glass so when it gets to Wasque the sheer volume of water pushes past at speeds sometimes up to five knots as it continues out to sea in a south/southwesterly direction. As it flushes past Wasque it deposits the sand and debris picked up along the way to form a series of shoals stretching all the way to Muskeget Channel, eight miles south. These shoals begin at Wasque Point and the combination of shoals, fast water and bait being swept through the sound is a perfect spot for hungry gamefish to sit and wait for dinner.

Because of its reputation and relative easy access, most first time visiting surfcasters headed to Wasque Point and I was no exception. There were two ways to get there. One way was to take a short trip on the On-Time ferry to Chappy, then drive the five miles to the Fishermen's parking lot and finally a short walk got you to the beach. But this was for the pilgrims who didn't own an ORV. If you were fortunate enough to own one you could purchase the required vehicle permit and access it via Norton Point, also known as South Beach, which was owned by Dukes County. Once you got onto Chappaquiddick you were then obligated to purchase a second permit from The Trustees of Reservations. This permit not only got you access to Wasque but the rest of the Chappaquiddick beaches that stretched from Metcalf's Hole, past Wasque, north to the Cape Poge lighthouse, then in a southwesterly direction toward the Windmill House, finally reaching land's end at the Gut. If I remember correctly the total cost of the two permits at the time was approximately $100 for the season.

I purchased the necessary permits and was on my way to the fabled Wasque Rip. On my very first trip along South Beach I hadn't gone more than a mile before I happened upon a school of breaking bluefish without another angler in sight. Birds were working and fish were crashing bait and hungry for my Atom popper - and I had them to myself! I had never encountered anything quite like this before and could not believe my good luck. When the action slowed, I continued my quest to Wasque, only to run into another school of blues a mile further down the beach. Again, not another soul in sight-how could this be? The action slowed again and when I finally got to the Rip, I found out why....

There had to be at least fifty vehicles parked side by side and sixty to seventy anglers at the surf and most had bent rods. Blues were lying dead or dying everywhere and anglers, some young, some old, some in waders or hip boots, and others in bare feet, were having a ball hooking bluefish after bluefish that ranged up to ten pounds. Some were using Kastmasters or Hopkins type lures while others were throwing Atom poppers. Still others were using a strange kind of tear drop type lure that I had never seen before and guys using that lure appeared to be out casting and out fishing everyone else. One guy using a conventional outfit kept running back and forth between the surf and his vehicle constantly changing lures and asking all those around him whether they were using "wood or metal, wood or metal?" Bluefish littered the beach. A bunch of buddies fishing together had stacked the fish in a mound that had to be close to three feet high and six or seven feet around. Bluefish were smashing this strange lure and just about everything else anglers were throwing. There was a lot of hooting and hollering going on and a lot of 'high fiving' and it was exciting as hell. Once in a while a loud 'snap' would resonate as an angler put too much into the cast and the lure went flying to parts unknown.

I often used to wonder where the thousands of cast off lures ended up and figured there must have been a lure haven somewhere along the south shore. I mentioned it one day while talking with Fred Moscolo of Trader Fred's surplus store. He told me that he and some friends went scuba diving at the Rip one time during slack tide and found a wadded up ball of lures about the size of a Volkswagen bug. He said they tried to get a line from a winch on it but the tide started moving and they just didn't have enough time to get it done.

Still others were swearing because of fish lost to frayed monofilment line. Some guys were out-fishing others and hardly anyone was releasing fish. The tide was running hard in a south westerly direction and arguments ensued as anglers didn't walk their fish down the beach with the current, or refused to do so which resulted in tangled lines, short tempers and lost fish. It was a wild scene and certainly unlike anything I had ever experienced. I was mesmerized and watched in amazement, a little afraid to wade into the fracas.

When I asked a guy standing in front of the vehicle next to me how long it had been going on he said at least forty-five minutes. I also learned that this was not unusual for Wasque Point in late September. As it turned out, the angler I spoke to was Arnold Spofford who had invented that strange looking tear drop shaped lure he called a Ballistic Missile. In 1988 Bob Post, a local dentist and surfcaster wrote *Reading the Water*, a terrific book about island surfcasters in which he profiled the top island surf anglers. Arnold Spofford was one of them. When I later asked Mr. Spofford to sign my copy of the book, he asked "what do you want me to write?"

I replied "lie like hell." He wrote: "To Ron, we taught each other all we know about fishing."

After about another half hour or so, the tide started to slow as did the action. Guys were also getting tired and the line of casters thinned so I decided it was a good time to try my luck. I clipped on my Atom popper and put all I could into my cast. I heard that terrible 'snap' and out to sea went the popper. Embarrassed, I slunk back to my vehicle to tie on another leader but by the time I got back to the surf, the tide had gone completely slack and the action had ended.

I hung around for awhile and made some more casts but the tide had changed direction and no one seemed interested in fishing anymore. Some loaded their fish into coolers and took off for home, while others cleaned their fish right on the beach heaving the carcasses into the Rip. Still others jumped in their vehicles and headed in a northerly direction toward Cape Poge. I talked to a few guys that were hanging around and tried to pick up whatever information I could. The most important thing I learned was that the best time to fish the Rip was about an hour after the current turned to the west and a southwesterly wind blowing against the west running tide usually produced the best action. When the current ran in an easterly direction which was a rising tide, the action was usually much slower or non-existent. I also learned that early in the tide, the best way to catch a bluefish was with a sinking lure like a Kastmaster or Hopkins but when things really heated up, a switch to a popper or Ballistic Missile was just as effective and definitely more fun. But Mr. Spofford also shared the knowledge that when the fish were blitzing like that the bigger fish hung near the bottom so even the inventor of the Ballistic Missile usually stayed with the metal lure and fished it very slowly. I don't remember anyone even mentioning the Derby.

I once asked Mr. Spofford what his favorite color 'Missile' was. He said he didn't have one and wasn't big on colors. He said colors were for catching fishermen not fish because "fish don't carry wallets."

The next day I checked the tide and planned my arrival about an hour after the tide change, just like the man said. I also hoped to get there early enough to get a good spot on the picket line I was sure would develop. But things had changed. A weather system was moving through and the bright almost balmy weather of the day before had given way to an overcast cold and gray day with the wind blowing from the northeast and building in strength.

I arrived at the Rip and was surprised to find that there was nowhere near the number of anglers or vehicles as the day before. The northeast wind had changed the beautiful fishy looking rip of the day before and there were a lot of people just hanging around. Hardly anyone was fishing and there were no bent rods. Undaunted, I decided to try my luck anyway. I clipped on my Kastmaster and started casting. I cast for almost two hours but my efforts produced only two fish on successive casts about an hour after I started. I saw only a few other fish caught and many people had left or just sat in their vehicles but every time a fish would get caught guys would grab their rods, and almost in formation, march to the beach and start casting thinking it was the start of another blitz. It was a scene that would become a very familiar sight over the years. But the blitz failed to materialize and most guys, including myself, simply gave up.

That storm blew for the rest of my brief stay on the Vineyard and the bluefishing about ground to a halt as well, so I used the next few days to explore and become familiar with the rest of the Chappaquiddick beaches.

I learned that a few hundred yards northeast of Wasque was a spot the locals called Leland's Beach named after the Leland family that owned the beach as well as the small house overlooking Wasque Point.

In the late eighties the property was taken by the state through eminent domain and then turned over to The Trustees of Reservations to manage.

The current here runs in a north-south direction instead of the southwesterly direction at the Rip. It's also not as shoaled up as Wasque and consequently a little deeper. Also, unlike the Rip, it produced fish on both tides. Five hundred yards north of Leland's is a spot called the 'snow fence'. There appears to be a shoal here and when the tide floods, or runs in a northerly direction, the bluefish sometimes school up to wait for dinner and there were always a few bait dunkers staked out there, particularly on the rising tide. A mile or so north of the snow fence and out in front of Dike Bridge was another good spot that also produced on both tides. Guys referred to this area simply as Dike Bridge or Tom's Shoal.

Continuing on the beach in a northerly direction for another mile would bring you to Arruda Point which I learned was named after George and Joan Arruda who 'owned' the spot for years before they just suddenly stopped fishing altogether.

Still further north are two small perpendicular rock piles called the jetties. The jetties are the remains of a breachway that in 1946 was cut through to Cape Poge pond to shorten the trip of boaters returning to Edgartown Harbor. Prior to that and again today, returning boaters would have to make a big loop around a shallow and shoaled Cape Poge point. The breachway cut at least two miles off the trip. Unfortunately, it was not maintained and filled in within two years but to this day it remains a favorite fishing hole.

Continuing north along Cape Poge for another quarter mile brings you to the northern most point of Chappaquiddick, with a lighthouse on the bluff warning mariners off the shoal below which extends northward toward the Cape.

Once you round Cape Poge point you start travelling in a southwesterly direction for a few miles until you finally run out of drivable beach at the Gut which is where Poucha Pond ebbs and flows in and out of Edgartown Harbor. Along the way from the Cape Poge lighthouse you pass by a lot of fishable water with landmarks called the Chimneys, the Elbow, the Windmill House, and Jared's Rock, finally arriving at the Gut.

As I explored the area I found guys fishing at most of these places, but during the weeklong storm the only place I caught fish other than the Wasque Rip was the Gut and it quickly became a favorite spot for me. It was a long way from the OSV point of access on South Beach in Edgartown but was relatively uncrowded and very fishable. I also learned that it was accessible from both sides of the narrow sixty yard by two hundred yard sluice. Access to the opposite, or southern side, was at North Neck Road off the paved Chappaquiddick Road.

During my travels that week I spoke to a lot of anglers but don't remember one of them mentioning the Derby, but the day I left I picked up a copy of the Vineyard Gazette which had a story about one of the participants as well as a list of the current leaders.

I returned the following year but because of my rowing commitment had only a few days to spend fishing. Once again, the Rip was on fire and I never made it past there but I used my down time to explore the rest of the island a little. I found my way along the south side of the island to Gay Head via Moshups Trail and then to Menemsha. The more I saw of Martha's Vineyard in the off season, the more I liked it. It had just about everything New England had to offer without the crowds and traffic, and the beaches and coastal views were stunning. It didn't take me long to set a goal of retiring there someday.

The colorful clay formations and the panorama from the top of the Gay Head Cliffs was an unbelievable sight and down below guys were fishing. I made my way over to the fishing village of Menemsha and again was taken by the sight of this picturesque fishing village. I learned that much of the classic Jaws movie had been filmed there and found the cottage that was used as Quint's fishing shack. Across the channel were the remains of the Orca, on its side and rotting away. Years later I learned that the area was a hot spot for stripers.

The entrance to Menemsha Harbor was a narrow, fast moving channel about eighty feet across and sixty yards long which opened on the east side to a large dock area and mooring field as well as the village of Menemsha. The channel continued in a southerly direction past a very long dock and a large red roofed Coast Guard Station at the end. Coast Guard vessels were docked on the east side of the dock. Just opposite the Coast Guard Station was a small inlet called the Menemsha Small Boat Basin. The channel then continued further south until it opened into the expanse of Menemsha Pond.

The current was moving out of the harbor and zipping through the channel at a speed of at least four knots and there were anglers with what looked like heavier fresh water rods fishing on the rocky jetties that bordered the sides. There were also a few boats out front as well as a lone angler fishing from a canoe out-rigged with life preservers for balance and floatation. I learned a few years later that the guy in the canoe was the legendary Roberto Germani.

I walked out on the Menemsha side of the jetty just in time to see all hell break loose as fish broke between the two jetties and guys from both sides started casting at them. Someone quickly hooked up and the fish took off out of the harbor carrying at least three lines along with it. Thinking the fish was his, one of the anglers on the opposite or Lobsterville side of the jetty reared back to set the hook and snapped his monofilament line as well as the line of the guy with the fish. A profanity laced exchange was hurled back and forth across the narrow inlet as the fish broke again just outside the harbor. This time anglers from both sides hooked up and the fish took off peeling line and heading for the Elizabeth Islands. I had never seen a bluefish run that fast or for so long and when I said something to that effect to the guy standing next to me he informed me they were false albacore or "little tunny." I had never even heard of a false albacore let alone catch one.

It took the guy about fifteen minutes to work the fish to the outside of the jetty and land it. It was the first time I had ever been close to any kind of tuna and I thought it was just beautiful. The fish weighed about eight pounds and I was taken by the green-blue iridescent color as well as the shape of it. The guy that caught it was ecstatic and quickly ran off the jetty and threw it in his cooler. All I thought about was how good it must taste and I wanted to catch one but wasn't about to get on that jetty with my eight foot surf rod which was the smallest I had. Instead I just observed the goings on and asked a few questions.

Most anglers were throwing very small lures but a few were using live mackerel. One of the lures was called a Swedish Pimple and someone told me it was a great lure for catching perch and jigging for walleyes in the Midwest. Another lure was a small needlefish and I was told that Arnold Spofford made this one as well. I also learned that the way to fish these lures was to retrieve them as fast as possible.

The fish broke yet again and another angler hooked up almost immediately. The crash of the fish on the lure was incredible. Again I watched him quickly work his way to the end of the jetty to fight the fish as he went over and under the picket line of guys who continued to cast. By this time the fish were also breaking just outside the entrance and a couple of guys in the boats had hooked up as well. A minute later the guy fighting the fish at the end of the jetty yelled an obscenity and just stood there staring down at his reel. He had gotten spooled! As he walked by me he kept muttering "I can't believe it, I can't believe that happened!"

The guy that ran the first fish off the beach had returned but took the time to talk with me for a while. He explained that the fish was almost totally inedible but big enough to weigh in for the 'Derby.' He was surprised, almost shocked, when I told him I had never heard of a false albacore and was even more surprised that I knew almost nothing about the Derby. He told me a little about the event and that his fish was not going to be a contender but might be big enough to win a daily pin. He then proceeded to show me the silver 'albie' pin he already had on his hat. He further explained there were five eligible species: striped bass, bluefish, weakfish, false albacore, and bonito, and there was a boat and shore category and that at the end of the event the anglers who caught the largest of all five were eligible to win the grand prize, which at the time, was a fully equipped Boston Whaler. He also explained that there were three daily winners in each species category and in addition to a pin the angler won a small monetary prize.

Just about then the fish blew up again and he rushed to find a spot on the jetty. I continued to watch the action for awhile but the current flowing out of the channel was slowing and with it the fishing, but my interest was piqued. I'm competitive by nature and love competition of almost any kind and I needed to find out more about the Derby. My problem was that I had committed to a rowing event that weekend and my brief vacation was over the next day. Once again I picked up a copy of the Gazette on my way off the Island and quickly flipped the pages until I found the weekly Derby results. I thought, "I need to enter this thing."

I did come back the following year and I did enter the Derby. I went to Dick's Bait and Tackle, picked up my Derby badge and number as well as a hat and program and thought, wow this is pretty cool, all this for the fifteen dollar entry fee. I even entered a fish that year, a nine-something pound bluefish that I caught during a blitz at Wasque. The whole thing at the Derby Headquarters was very impressive and I felt pretty special slapping my fish on the table and picking up my official weigh-in slip. A few days later I read the Gazette and saw my name listed as winner of a daily Mystery Prize. Since I hadn't read all the rules, I had no clue what a Mystery Prize was but when I inquired about it at the weigh station, I was surprised and pleased when they handed me a nice canvas bag emblazoned with the Derby logo and loaded with more than $100 worth of line, lures and other goodies. They told me it was a luck-of-the-draw prize for anyone that enters a fish and there was a Mystery Prize for each species. This was getting better all the time. A lot of the guys weighing fish that night had pins on their hats and I wanted one very badly.

I was also starting to meet more people and recognize some faces and buggies from the prior two years. In addition, out on Chappy, I was starting to expand my horizon by moving around a little more rather than concentrate all my efforts at Wasque Point. I arrived at the Cape Poge jetties at sunrise one morning to find a bunch of guys casting to breaking fish. A couple were right on the end of the south jetty, a couple on the small beach between the jetties and one on the north side. They all seemed to be together and they were furiously casting with tackle that appeared to be a lot smaller than what I had seen being used for bluefish at the Rip. Occasionally fish would break and birds would descend upon a very small area and the guys would feverishly cast into it, but nobody was hooking up. What was going on, didn't bluefish hit just about anything that moved? Even the anglers in the three or four boats out front were not hooking up.

When things finally slowed, I introduced myself to one of the guys. His name was Ernie Baracchini and he told me these fish were either bonito or false albacore which I had seen the year before at Menemsha. He also told me that most of the guys there were either his brothers or related. Later I met Kenny, Phil and John Baracchini and their brother in law Dick Adams. Over the years we all became good friends and most of them continue to fish the Derby, some with their sons who were just toddlers then or hadn't even been born.

I also continued to see Mr. Spofford as well as another old timer who I learned was Art Winters, also known as "Bonito" Art because of his ability to catch bonito.

Out at the Rip there were Peter and Paul Bergeron aptly dubbed the "Twin Towers" because of their six foot four height. Along with Jeff (Cowboy) Leistyna, another six-four guy who always wore a cowboy hat, they took up a lot of room but also seemed to catch more bluefish than everyone else.

There was "Ev" from New Hampshire, an older gray haired guy and a real gentleman. Ev owned a similarly old but beautifully clean and rust free Jeep Wagoneer that had its chrome bumpers almost totally covered with colorful OSV beach permits from Norton Point and Chappaquiddick.

I met Artie, Orest, Rogie, and Dave, who were the guys that liked to keep everything they caught and the ones who stacked their blue-fish on the beach like cordwood. Great guys, but I could never fig-ure out why they kept so many fish!

Lance and Lois Dimock are from Bolton, CT. They came up on va-cation in July of 1987 and Lance borrowed some fishing equipment and went to the Wasque Rip. In the middle of a bluefish blitz he caught a striper on a Roberts Ranger. He had never seen a striper before in his life. The fish weighed 50 lbs..

A few years later in 1991 he caught a 42 lb. striper under the Cape Poge lighthouse on a 2oz. Hopkins. It was one of the years stripers were removed from the Derby.

In 1994 while fishing at the Rip, Lois caught a 16.25 lb. bluefish that was good for third place in the All Tackle Shore Bluefish Division. The winning fish that year was 16.56 lbs..

Lance and Lois still return to fish the Derby for a week every year and Lois has won more Mystery Prizes than anyone I know.

There was Mark Carlson from Waterbury, CT. Mark was a throw-back from the sixties complete with a hairy little goatee, mustache and tie-dye T-Shirts. During the 1988 Derby, in the middle of a blue-fish blitz and casting shoulder to shoulder with 50 other guys, Mark caught a fifty-three inch, fifty one pound striper on a 4 oz. Kastmaster. He said the fish hit as soon as the lure hit the water, like it was waiting with its mouth open. He attempted to revive it for release but the fish kept turning belly up so he kept it and to get an accurate weight weighed it at Derby headquarters knowing full well it was a year in which stripers were not eligible for prizes. Later, he had Derby Hall of Famer and Island taxidermist Janet Messineo mount the fish for him. He took a picture of it with a red Santa Claus hat on its head and the next year sent out Merry 'Bassmas' cards.

Mark just recently started fishing the Derby again after a long absence. He looks exactly the same, right down to the goatee and shirts. He says he was not the least bit disappointed that his 'fifty' was ineligible for a Derby prize as it remains one of the highlights of his life and the attention he got from the experience led him to meet new people and develop friendships that have lasted for more than twenty five years.

Dan and Mary Ellen Stiles were friends of Mark's from Nyack, NY and the owners of two beautiful German Shepards that always accompanied them on their fishing trips to the beach. They were regular visitors during the Derby and Dan was a consistent prize winner until he moved to the island permanently a few years back. He works so many hours as a line manager for NSTAR now that we rarely see him on the beach.

There was an attractive woman with great legs who always wore a blue bandana on her head and fished barefoot in cutoff jeans. She was obviously a regular out there and could handle a fishing rod and hold her own with the best of the guys. I learned years later it was Shirley Prada Craig who was a native islander and married to the late Phil Craig, author of the Vineyard Mystery series of books. Shirley and Phil also co-authored: *"Delish"* The J. W. Jackson Cookbook.

I met the Zanes family from New Jersey. Brothers Charlie and Newt, and Charlie's sons Rick, Dave and Rob. These guys just loved to catch bluefish! When I first met them, Charlie and Newt were in their fifties and the boys in their twenties. The Zanes didn't get into the Derby all that much but every year would plan a two week stay around the prime spring bluefishing and spend all day, every day, rain or shine, on the beach catching bluefish. They would count the number of fish they caught and many years the count ran into the thousands but only a few would be kept which Charlie would serve for dinner. The appetizer was usually 'bluefish fingers.'

One year I ran into them on East Beach. It was almost dark and the fishing had been red hot for the entire tide. Most guys had caught their fill, but Rick and Dave couldn't get enough and continued to hammer fish on almost every cast, while Charlie, being every bit the patient father, was leaning against the side of the truck with his arms folded, obviously ready to leave. But the two adult boys were like excited twelve year olds having fun at an amusement park, only instead of asking to go on one more ride, were pleading with Charlie for "one more cast Dad, one more cast!"

There was a jovial guy who seemed to befriend everyone on the beach. It was Don Mohr, who later became the Derby chairman and a very close friend of mine. The Zanes family dubbed him "Coach."

A good friend of Don's was an Englishman by the name of Gordon Ditchfield.

There were others and I learned that some of them were very successful businessmen and leaders in their respective fields. But it didn't matter who you were or what your lot in life was, when you were fishing at the Rip, the name of the game was bluefish and the goal was winning the Derby.

As the years passed, I would see most of these people as well as many others on a regular basis. I was also starting to learn that 'camaraderie' as Don Mohr liked to put it, was a very important part of the Derby experience.

Also, over the next few years, I learned that there was more to life than bluefish and became a rabid bonito and false albacore angler.

I still fished the madness at the Rip but started having trouble fishing among the multitude of anglers and the craziness that occurred there on a regular basis. More and more I was drawn to the jetties and what went on there.

The jetties seemed to be the place on Chappy to catch false albacore and bonito and after a year or two of trying unsuccessfully to catch these fish I started arriving at sunrise along with the Baracchini crowd. They taught me that the way to go was a #7 Swedish Pimple or a light green colored one ounce Spofford Needlefish. They told me to rip them across the surface on the retrieve and that seemed to be effective as they caught a fair number of fish that way. On the back of the package of Mr. Spofford's needlefish he stated *"retrieve this lure as fast as you can, if they want it, they'll get it."* It was good advice then and it's still good advice today! Not much in surfcasting can compare to the explosion of a false albacore or bonito hitting a lure on the surface.

The area was often loaded with three-inch sand eels and the fish would work a pattern as they moved down the beach from the direction of the Cape Poge lighthouse to the jetties crashing for a few seconds, sounding, then reappearing and sounding again. A cast into the middle of the breaking fish would sometimes produce a smashing hit as an angler would hook up and walk the fish out of the way of other fishermen who, for the most part, were respectful of the guy with the fish and not cast over him or near his running fish. There were times when the breaking fish were albies but also times when they were bonito or bluefish.

In the very early days and because most guys had limited experience with these speedsters, many people, myself included, had problems telling the difference between false albacore and bonito. When anglers started to discover this fishery, there were even magazine articles describing how to identify one from the other. Also, there were no Shimano high retrieve ratio reels or Loomis light weight rods so my first efforts were with the heaviest freshwater rod and reel I owned.

My first experience with a "fast fish" was at the jetties right about the time of a glorious sunrise into a bright red sky when an albie smashed my light green Spofford needlefish about twenty yards from the beach. I had watched other guys fight their fish but was unprepared for what happened next. After the initial smash, the fish swam toward me for a few seconds then took off on a screaming run away from the beach and for what seemed like an eternity, the likes of which I had never experienced before. I could not believe how fast the 10# mono disappeared off my small Mitchell 300 freshwater spinning reel. My heart was pounding, my knees went weak and

I actually started shaking. I kept repeating a prayer to the fish gods "God, please don't let me lose this fish, please don't let me lose this fish!" It's a prayer that I would repeat many times in the next few years as every time I hooked one of those fish and felt their power and speed then stood helpless as the line flew off the small reel, the feeling would return again and the prayer would start all over.

I was fully focused on landing this fish and after a few more heart stopping runs and a 100 yard walk up the beach, I carefully dragged it up on the sand. A beautiful football-shaped false albacore. I was thrilled; this fish was going to the weigh-in that night. I was also mentally and emotionally drained and just stood there looking at the fish, admiring its beauty and thinking about what had just taken place. When I finally got around to removing the small treble hooks from its toothless mouth and looked around, I saw a couple of the Baracchini gang walking fish up the beach toward me and the rest of the gang with rods at the ready, waiting for fish to break again. And the sun had been up for less than an hour! I knew I was hopelessly addicted. This was something entirely different and exciting to me. I was still interested in catching bluefish, but catching these speed-sters was going to be a new Derby priority for me.

FALSE ALBACORE, BONITO AND MORE BLUEFISH

I CONTINUED TO return to the Vineyard on a regular basis, vacationing with my family in the summer and returning to fish the Derby in the fall. In the summer, the primary target was bluefish at the Rip and during daily visits to South Beach my son Ron and I would leave my wife and daughters somewhere along the beach and continue on to Wasque where many times it was non-stop action, even in August. Blitzes were not uncommon and we would have a ball bailing on fish. As my kids got a little older they would sometimes bring friends who had never held a fishing rod before in their lives, and after some short lessons, they would catch fish.

In the fall I would return for a week to go on the hunt for a Derby winner and for the next eight or ten years rarely remember even a daily skunking.

The day would usually start before dawn and even with the long drive down South Beach around Wasque Point then down East Beach to the jetties, I was usually at the end of the south jetty when the first light showed in the east and most times the fish would show shortly after I arrived. After my first experience with a false alba-core I added an eight foot fiberglass rod and a Penn 4400S reel to my fishing arsenal. It wasn't the ideal set-up and really didn't throw light weight lures all that far, but it got the job done.

A couple of years later Shimano came out with a line of smaller high-speed reels and I bought the low end Symetre with a retrieve ratio of 6.1 in relation to the slower 4.1 ratio of most of the Penn reels. From everything I had read up to that time, the faster you could crank a reel, the better your chances of success were to catch one of these green speedsters, and this reel put more speed into the equation.

About the same time I saw a 'How To' article in the *New England Fisherman* that described how to build a seven foot graphite 'Red Fin' (weakfish) rod. Rod blanks were transitioning from fiberglass to graphite at the time and there were some reservations among veteran surf anglers about the use of graphite. Many thought graph-ite would turn brittle in colder weather and break easily but the rod seemed like it would be perfect for albies and bones so I took a chance and asked my brother to build one for me. It was a Fisher blank and I asked him to use cork rings on the grips above and be-low the reel seat. I love that rod and it served me well up until about three years ago when I finally retired it out of fear that I might break it. Over the years I had it re-wrapped at least three times and made so many casts with it, there is now a smooth indentation in the cork where I gripped the rod.

—⊶⊷—

In the mid to late eighties when you fished the jetties and points north, as well as the Gut, you were targeting bonito and false albacore. Many times you really didn't know what you were going to catch, as there was usually a mixed bag of fish chasing the big schools of sand eels that frequented the area. Some days you'd be standing on the jetties and look north to see birds working over breaking fish that had bait trapped right up against the beach and moving against the tide toward the jetties. When you got a cast into them, you had to be prepared to hook one of the targeted speedsters, a bluefish, or on occasion, even a Spanish mackerel.

Late one stormy afternoon with a strong Northeast wind blowing against a flooding tide, I was the only angler on the jetties and hooked up eight bonito. I got clobbered by waves breaking over the jetty and was soaking wet and cold, but I didn't care, I was catching bonito - and a lot of them!

On another occasion, I was just relaxing on the beach at Arruda Point when some bait sprayed within casting range. I made a cast with a Spofford needlefish and it came back loaded with sandeels impaled on the small trebles. Just for the heck of it, I threw it back out, made one crank on the reel and a big bonito inhaled it. That fish was 8.5 lbs..

I bought my house on the Vineyard in 1990 and that fall, after spending ten days fishing the Derby by myself, I joined my son Ron and his friends for a few more days and we had some pretty good success catching bonito and false albacore. Very early one morning we made the long trip along South Beach and arrived at the North Neck side of the Gut and started tossing eels. Just as it started to get light, some fish crashed and three of us had pick-ups and felt our eels go racing toward the eastern end of the Gut. When we set the hooks there was resistance for a second and then nothing - they were gone. False albacore had picked up our eels.

That same year, while fishing at Arruda's our family friend Dan Segee caught a nine pound bonito and Ron an eight pounder. For some reason Dan hadn't entered the Derby that year. Had he done so, his fish would have taken second place in the All Tackle Shore Bonito Division. Ron's fish won a gold pin that day!

Don't misunderstand me, the fish weren't always blitzing and the fishing wasn't always good. In 1994 I fished the Derby for eleven days and caught five striped bass, two bluefish, four albies and no bonito.

1995 was worse! Over ten days I caught four stripers, one bluefish and one false albacore, and didn't get to the weigh-in once.

In 1996 I again joined Ron and his friends for five days early in the Derby and caught one striper, one small albie, a surprise keeper fluke at the Rip, and only five bluefish, all of which were caught in a forty five minute span. But there were some big bluefish around that year and even though one of my fish was just under thirteen pounds, I didn't even score a daily pin with it.

During one trip that year, Ron, Dan Segee, Emilio Galindo, Phil Hennig, and I started fishing at 5:00 AM. We fished our way along South Beach, stopped at the Rip, fished all the usual places along East Beach, stopped at the jetties, both sides of the Windmill House, and finally ended at the Gut where we stayed for a while. In almost six hours, the four of us didn't even have a hit let alone catch a fish and hadn't talked with anyone who did, but when we got back to East Beach around noon, there were bluefish slicks everywhere and hardly a soul on the beach. We bailed out of our vehicles, made a cast and hooked up almost immediately. I had on a two-ounce fluorescent green Gibbs needlefish which I didn't bother to change and nailed a big bluefish. At the same time Dan, who after his previous mistake, decided to enter the Derby that year, hooked up on a big fish as well. I landed my fish and by the time I got it back to the car and threw the fish in the cooler, Dan's fish had taken him about 200 yards up the beach toward Wasque. I watched for a minute or so as he continued the trek, then started the car and went after him.

The fish was only a few yards off the beach but Dan could do nothing with it and it was obvious his drag was set way too loose, as he could not muscle it onto the sand. As I drove along beside him, I suggested that he tighten his drag but the old advice about not tightening the drag when on a fish, stuck in his head and he refused to do it. By now, he was at least a quarter of a mile from where he had started. I finally stopped the car, got out, and started walking with him. I said something like, "Dan, tighten that damn drag and get that fish on the beach, it's probably dead by now anyway." He hesitated a bit and walked a few more steps before he tightened the drag and slid the fish onto the sand.

We each caught a few more before the action slowed and couldn't believe our good fortune at being the only ones into fish. We figured we had four daily winners and couldn't wait to get to the weigh-in that night. When we arrived shortly after eight there was already a line of guys waiting to weigh bluefish. It seemed there had been a full scale blitz going on at the Rip for an hour before we got to East Beach. Of our group, Dan's was the biggest at 13.98 lbs. and he tied for the daily gold pin but took home the prize because he weighed his in first. He also ended the day in third place in the Shore All Tackle Bluefish Division, but unfortunately didn't stay in that position for more than a day or two. The rest of us all had fish over ten pounds but were well out of pin contention.

I came back for the last week of the Derby that year and did a little better on bass but caught nothing worth weighing. I also did not

catch an albie or bonito and only a couple of small bluefish, but while I was on the Island, Jack Livingston caught a 9.42 lb. bonito at the Cape Poge crossover on a 1 oz. Hammer. The fish was a Grand Leader. The Grand Leader shore bluefish that year was caught on Chappy by Dennis Williams. The fish weighed 18.47 lbs.

As slow as the fishing could be at times back then, there always seemed to be a run of big bluefish somewhere on Chappy. In 1992, Larry Mercier was a Grand Leader with a seventeen pound fish caught during a blitz at the Rip.

In 1995, Lori Vanderlaske caught an 18.69 lb. Grand Leader bluefish, reportedly at the Gut.

In 1998, a few years after his son Dennis caught his eighteen-pound fish, Abe Williams caught a 20.58 lb. bluefish 'somewhere' on Chappy and was a Grand Leader.

In 1999, Paul Schultz, who was also profiled in Robert Post's *Reading the Water*, was fishing the Rip along with a number of other guys. They were doing well on bluefish when two whales cruised through and the action ended. In an attempt to find the fish again, Paul said most guys moved west toward Metcalf's Hole but he and John Schillinger moved in the opposite direction toward Leland's Point. Paul caught a 14.92 lb. bluefish on a Chrome Roberts Ranger and was a Grand Leader.

Two years later in 2001 I was on East Beach one afternoon when bluefish blitzed along the entire stretch from in front of Dike Bridge all the way to the Rip. Jack Livingston lives on Chappy and at the time was a chef at the Black Dog and helped put together the Black Dog Cook Book. If you are ever lucky enough to catch a rare bonito, his recipe for 'Bubba's (Bill Clinton) Bonito' is on page 136. Jack likes to fish early in the morning and rarely fishes in the afternoon or evening but acted on a hunch that day and drove out to the beach in the middle of the afternoon. He caught a 15.26 lb. Grand Leader bluefish! My biggest that day was over twelve pounds and didn't come close to winning a daily pin, let alone make it onto the leader board.

Although 2001 seemed to mark the end of the blitzes, Derby shore division winners continue to be caught on Chappy. In 2002, Dan Geary made a lucky cast with a borrowed Atom Popper and caught a 15.69 lb. fish that was a Grand Leader.

In 2003 Tom Kieras was a Grand Leader after he chunked up a 15.27 lb. bluefish.

Bob (Bubba) McKay and Ron (Sully) Sullivan are Derby fishing partners who primarily target false albacore when they are here for their annual two week stay. In 2005 the albie fishing was so bad they decided to go to what they refer to as the 'dark side' and chunked bait one afternoon. Sully caught a 13.70 lb. bluefish and was a Grand Leader. They probably haven't gone to the 'dark side' three times since!

And finally, in 2013 Ralph Peckham was a Grand Leader with a 15.18 lb. fish.

Ironically, with all of the Grand Leaders that have been caught on Chappy over the years, only Tom Kieras has been lucky enough to win the Grand Prize.

DON MOHR

READER'S DIGEST MAGAZINE used to run a monthly feature titled 'The Most Unforgettable Character I Ever Met.' In thirty plus years of Derby participation I've been fortunate enough to have met two people who I could easily say fit that special distinction. One of them was Don Mohr. Don was one of the mentally and physically toughest, yet the most open and congenial soul I've ever had the pleasure of knowing.

Before I actually met him, I had often seen him at the Wasque Rip shaking hands and greeting just about everyone out there as though they were his best friend, but my first real contact with him came as I was driving down South Beach one afternoon on my way home after fishing a particularly good dropping tide at the Rip. I looked in my rear view mirror and saw this brown pick-up barreling down the beach toward me way above the unofficial speed limit of fifteen miles per hour. I thought wow, this guy either has a big fish or had way too much to drink.

As he got closer I pulled slightly off to the right thinking he was going to pass but instead he pulled alongside and motioned for me to stop. I had no clue as to what he might want, but as it turned out, he was leaving the Rip and found a surf rod with a Penn 704 lying in the sand and wanted to know if I had all my rods. After a quick check of my roof rack, I determined that none were missing and we had a brief discussion about how good the fishing was and off he went. I remember thinking what a good guy he was!

The next day at the Rip he was there and in his usual fashion joking and talking with everyone he came in contact with. When I asked someone who the guy was, I was told he was the athletic director at Ohio State University and the guy who had recently fired the famous football coach, Woody Hayes. I learned much later that he was in fact an athletic director not at Ohio State but at Wright State University, a smaller, lesser known school outside of Dayton, OH.

While at Wright State, Don started fourteen varsity sports and took the school to Division I status. He was also responsible for setting up the first official training facility for the US Olympic Volleyball team.

Anchored by Captain Karsh Kiraly, the team won the first ever US gold medal in men's volley ball at the 1984 summer Olympics in Los Angeles.

During World War II he joined the Marines and saw action throughout the Pacific theater of war. He also played baseball for the Marine Corps baseball team and once played a game against an all star team that had both the legendary Joe DiMaggio in the outfield as well as future Hall of Fame pitcher Red Ruffing in the line-up. Early in the game Don hit a home run off Ruffing and as the teams were changing places after the inning, he and DiMaggio passed each other. DiMaggio congratulated him on the homer but warned him to be careful the next time up and sure enough, on his next at bat, Ruffing threw one right at his head.

Don was awarded a Purple Heart, not for a wound suffered in combat but a leg he broke while sliding into second base. While he was recuperating in the hospital tent, an officer walked in and proceeded down the row of cots throwing Purple Heart medals at the feet of the wounded marines. When the medal landed on Don's cot, he picked it up and tossed it back to him telling him he broke his leg playing baseball and didn't deserve it.

When it came time to depart the island on a troop ship that was anchored offshore he was told that because of his injury and leg cast, he couldn't leave because he would be unable to climb the rope ladder to the top of the railing. His reply was "the hell I can't" and with the help of his "Polish buddies'" who pushed and pulled him, he climbed to the top and over the railing, and was out of there.

After the war, he coached baseball and football at Cincinnati Reading High School as well as Wright State, and scouted for the Cincinnati Reds and the Brooklyn Dodgers. He was the first inductee into Wright State Sports Hall of Fame.

During his athletic career and subsequent retirement to the Vineyard, Don was plagued with back, knee, and hip problems and underwent seven back surgeries, four hip replacements and two knee surgeries. Athletes play with pain. Don Mohr fished with pain. There was so much scar tissue in his back from previous surgeries that during his last procedure, doctors had trouble inserting a needle to administer an epidural. After five attempts which caused a tremendous amount of pain and discomfort, Don told the anesthesiologist in no uncertain terms that he was giving him one more chance to get the needle in but if it didn't work, he was getting "the hell off the table and going home." They got it in!

After one of his hip replacements he developed a staph infection in the hip and the only way they could cure it was by removing it completely for a few months. So for three months, he had no hip at all.

In spite of all this, he rarely let it hinder his fishing and he never complained about the obvious pain he was in. Many times he could be seen standing at the edge of the surf with a rod in his hand, hunched over stretching out his back. Nothing was going to keep him off the beach and away from his friends and the thing he liked most in this world.

After one of his earlier hip operations, he was advised not to stand, not to wade, and not to wear heavy waders, but even that didn't dampen his enthusiasm, or deter him from fishing. He would carry an old plastic patio chair in the back of his pickup, drag it to the surf line and sit and cast. But the chair inhibited his casting so he would stand, make his cast and then sit down to retrieve or fight his fish if he hooked one, and there was always a friend or two around who were more than willing to help him land or unhook it for him.

When I first started fishing the Derby and weighed in a fish, the volunteers at the weigh-in would always ask where it was caught. Anglers being anglers, especially during the Derby, would rarely tell the truth and the most common answer was "South Beach" which encompasses more than twenty five miles of shore line. There were also answers like; in the mouth, in the water, out there, the Great Lakes, and other more creative and colorful replies.

In 1992 when the Derby Committee re-introduced striped bass as a Derby species after a seven-year hiatus, they did it unofficially, with little fanfare and a simple plaque being the only prize. Bob Lane caught a 51-pound fish that year and won the plaque. When they asked him where he caught his fish, Bob replied, "Carl's Rock." To this day, not many people know where Carl's Rock is but from that point on every time someone from Don's circle of friends weighed in a fish of any kind and asked where it was caught, the answer was "Don's Chair."

As age finally started taking its toll, instead of a chair he would carry a five gallon pail out to a beach, set a toilet seat on top and sit and cast from it. It didn't matter if he caught or not, it was important to him to be on the beach with his buddies.

When I first met Don in the early-eighties, in spite of his physical problems, one of his favorite places to fish was a rock at the end of the longer jetty on Cape Poge. There are really only two good rocks on that jetty that allow an angler to make a cast seaward toward breaking albies or bonito. One of them is slanted at a pretty severe angle with a flat portion at the very bottom that provides an area about the width of a size twelve boot, barely enough room for an angler to stand on. The other is a fairly flat rock. When a fish is hooked the drill is to hold on while the fish makes its run, hobble off the rock and then make your way down the jetty onto the sand where you can continue to fight and beach your fish. Somehow Don would get himself out to one of those rocks and that's where I really got to know him.

The bluefishing at Wasque was so good back then that most anglers hadn't discovered the fun and excitement of catching albies or bonito. In contrast to today when it's sometimes difficult to find a spot at the jetties to fish, the area was relatively uncrowded. Many times, Don and I would arrive around sunrise and have the place to ourselves until the blue fishermen, or those that sleep until the crack of noon, started to arrive. Even if he arrived late, or if someone else was there and hooked a fish, they would walk it off the rocks and out of respect tell him to take their spot.

He loved to catch 'bones' and albies and if there was no sign of fish at the jetties, he would often race off looking for them at Arruda's, the Gut or run all the way back to the Rip to fish for bluefish. If he didn't find fish at any of those places, he would come roaring back to the jetties and start all over again.

One year, when the Derby still awarded daily pins for false albacore, Don and I were fishing at Chappy Point Beach by the On Time Ferry slip. Action had been slow but all of sudden fish broke right in front of us and we simultaneously hooked up almost immediately. We dodged and weaved around each other as the fish ran in opposite directions but eventually beached the fish which were respectable enough to weigh in. It was around 9:30 AM and the last morning of my vacation. Don intended to head to East Beach for some bluefish action so he asked me if I would weigh his fish for him. We said our good-byes and I lined up for the ferry ride back to Edgartown and the weigh-in. When the albies were put on the scale they were exact twins to the one hundredth of a pound.

In those days there was no real-time information so the only way to know how you made out with your fish was to check the board outside the weigh-in station the next morning, or wait for the Gazette or Times to come out later in the week.

A few days later when the Gazette arrived at my house I immediately went to Mark Lovewell's column and checked the results to see if I had won a daily prize. To my dismay, I saw that Don's fish took a daily fourth but there was no mention of mine. As it turned out, when I weighed the fish, I had put Don's fish on the scale first and since it was a fourth place fish and there are no ties, Don's being the first on the scale, took the last daily prize.

I cut the results out of the paper and sent it to him along with a note that read something like 'we hooked up at the same time, we landed the fish at the same time, and they were exactly the same size, but because I was a gentleman and put your fish on the scale first, you won the pin. The least you could do is give me half of your prize.' A few days later, half of a five dollar Derby check along with a false albacore pin with the front end hack-sawed off arrived in the mail. I still have that pin and it's one of my most cherished Derby possessions.

Don Mohr loved the Derby and the people he met. He referred to the beach banter as "camaraderie." He also coveted the daily pins he won and like many pin winners displayed them proudly on his hat. On the beach every morning, the first words out of his mouth, whether he knew the angler or not, was usually "how ya doin ol' boy?" The next question was "well, did you make the board?" If he met someone new on the beach during the Derby, he would always leave with "hope you come in second."

His biggest Derby accomplishment came in 1984 when the Derby had separate divisions for residents and non-residents. One morning late in the Derby, he was casting a Hopkins at Quansoo and caught a forty-two pound fish that vaulted him into first place in the resident shore striped bass division. Around 1:00 AM a couple of nights later and during a howling nor-easter, there was a knock on his door and a very wet but very excited Chip Bergeron, a neighbor and friend, was standing in the doorway. Chip asked him to come out in the pouring rain to look at a fish. When Don peered into the truck bed he saw a big striper and disappointedly told Chip that he knocked him out of first place. As it turned out Chip hadn't become a permanent resident yet so his fish took the lead in the non-resident division.

Don ended up second in the Resident Shore Striped Bass Division that year and Chip held on to win the non-resident division. Chip eventually made a permanent move to the Vineyard and has distinguished himself as one of the Island's premier fly fishermen. He has won the Fly Rod Shore Bluefish Division twice, the Fly Rod Shore Striped Bass Division and currently holds the Fly Rod Shore Grand Slam record of 48.04 lbs., a feat he accomplished in one week.

Don served on the Derby committee from 1984 until 1991. He was treasurer from 1985 to 1989, and then took over as Chairman. During his tenure as Chairman, he helped the Derby transition from an event run by the Island Chamber of Commerce to an independent non-profit event. Also during his term, the committee enlisted the services of artist Ray Ellis to begin painting a series of scenes of well-known Island fishing locations.

Until he passed away in 2013, Ray Ellis prints graced the cover of the Derby program and were sold as a limited edition, numbered and highly collectible print, the proceeds of which were used to help fund the Derby scholarship program. In addition, the eight Grand Prize winners also received the first eight numbered prints which were personally signed and remarqued by Mr. Ellis.

The inaugural painting was done in 1988 and depicted four surf-casters at Wasque Point. It was beautifully painted with a milky blue sky, gently rolling surf and surfcasters with bent rods turned toward the southwest as they followed fish that ran with the current. One of them was painted wearing a yellow rain slicker and a matching yellow rain hat. Don always said it was him, and indeed, it did look like him.

Don once told me that if he ever became too disabled to fish he would still find a way to get himself to the beach just to see the people and enjoy the 'camaraderie'. As the years progressed and physical problems continued to take their toll, his strong will still brought him to the beach almost every day until the age of eighty three when he just couldn't get himself there anymore. Even then, his wife Marian and guys like Phil Horton and Bruce Erdman would bring him to the beach often, just to see his "ol' buddies."

Don was inducted into the Derby Hall of Fame in 2005 and the write up in the Derby program describes him as a beach ambassador who epitomizes what the Derby is all about. The program reads: "This sportsman always has a smile and helping hand for his fellow anglers."

He passed away in September 2012 at the age of eighty nine, and fittingly, during the Derby he loved so much. As a sign of respect, members of the Wright State football team wore his initials on their uniforms for the remainder of the season.

!n 1951, as a tribute to General Douglas MacArthur, a songwriter by the name of Frank Westphal wrote a song titled "Old Soldiers

Never Die, They Just Fade Away." I haven't heard that song since I was a very young boy but it was haunting and has stuck in my mind for all these years. When I remember it, I think of Don Mohr because that's exactly what happened to him. In my mind, he just faded away, and it's hard to believe that wonderful personality and strong physical presence is no longer in our midst.

THE VIAGRA
FISHING TEAM

Don Mohr was part of a group that the late Charlie Barr dubbed "The Viagra Fishing Team!" Although not a competitive team, the four good friends with diverse personalities and backgrounds formed quite the foursome on the Chappy beaches with fishing being the obvious common thread.

Marsh Bryan was a graduate of Princeton University and I never really knew what Marsh did for a living but was told he once owned a sporting goods store (or stores) somewhere in New Jersey, and that his father-in-law was a former Commodore of the prestigious New York Yacht Club, the founder of the America's Cup sailboat races.

Marsh was also the owner of a beautiful contemporary summer home on Chappaquiddick situated high on a hill with expansive million dollar views of Katama Bay and South Beach. He was a slender, straight and tall man and presented a striking figure on the beach.

If you are old enough to remember the Marlborough Man from the cigarette commercials, try to conjure up a picture of the guy leaning against a truck with a knee at an angle, a cigarette drooping from the corner of his mouth, but wearing a fishing cap instead of a cowboy hat, and you'll get an idea of what Marsh Bryan looked like. When I first met him in the mid nineties he had more than thirty years of surfcasting experience, most of it on the Vineyard.

⸺❋⸺

Gordon Ditchfield was a washashore from England and a retired correspondent for the Rueters News Agency. He was a little on the short side with thin gray hair and wore wire rimmed glasses that gave him the look of a respected newsman which is exactly what he was. As you would expect he was very articulate and spoke with a precise British accent. Gordon was a real gentleman and one of the few Englishmen I could understand. I enjoyed hearing him speak. As a rule, he didn't curse or use foul language and it always surprised me to the point of laughter when he unleashed the F-Bomb in that English accent, usually on his good buddy Don Mohr. You just didn't expect that word to come out of that gentlemanly mouth. He was also the last guy you would expect to find on the beach dunking bait on Cape Poge in the middle of the night or throwing a Roberts Rangers at the Wasque Rip.

I once asked him what his favorite Reuter's assignment was and without hesitation he told me it was the Olympics which he started covering in Melbourne in 1956. His career as part of a Reuter's team covering the Olympics also took him to games in Tokyo, Mexico City, Munich, and Montreal.

In 1968 Gordon also covered the Washington race riots and his son Michael related the following story.

"I knew the city better than he did and he asked me to drive him to where the city was burning. At 14th and U Street we reached a police line. We got out of the car (personally I wasn't keen on that idea, there was a lot of chaos, cops, smoke and angry people). He took out his press card and announced to the cops that he was going through. He was told that **nobody** *crossed the line. He argued very loudly that the press had a right to report the news and crossed the line. A very large cop slammed him up against a wall and said, "Nobody goes through here, black or white." Gordon's response to me after he was pushed back was: "Can you find us another way in?" I said, "There is no us, Dad."*

∽∾∾∽

Walter Lison was a former business executive who worked in the tough New York City garment district. He possessed a dry wit and was an avid outdoorsman who loved to duck hunt and fish. Before retiring to the Vineyard in 1992 he cut his surfcasting teeth on the rocks at Montauk Point and the beaches of Long Island. He was also a master rod builder and helped design the Van Staal reel, working with Rob Kowleyn to develop and bring it into production. He still owns a prototype VS 300 reel with serial #3. Out of the four, Walter was the true fisherman of the group.

On June 11, 1998, Walter and I shared an incredible fishing experience at the Edgartown Pond opening and I remember it clearly. The pond had been breached two days earlier and we agreed to fish it one morning. We arrived at the opening just as the sky started to lighten and surprisingly had the place to ourselves. The sky was cloudless, the winds light from the south, and there was a strong flow out of the pond which set up perfect conditions for what we were about to experience. We waded out on the bar that had built and hooked up on our first casts with blue and white Danny's and almost every cast after resulted in a mid-teen size striper. As the sky continued to brighten I started to see fish in the waves but when I mentioned it to Walter he said "nah, it's your imagination running wild." But as it got lighter there was no doubt and by the time the sun was over the horizon each breaking wave held a row of stripers three or four deep from the top to the bottom and across its entire width. I remember thinking it looked like an army of stripers.

There was no real aggression but the Danny wouldn't travel more than a few feet before a single fish would break out of the formation to pounce on the lure. If the first one missed it, another would be right there to take it. It was almost as if they were taking their turn and the best part was the way we could see the whole thing play out as if we were watching a movie in slow motion. The slower the retrieve the more time we had to watch and the movie lasted for a full ninety minutes until the tide changed and forced us off the bar. It was a surreal experience and the sight of those fish lined up in the waves is indelibly etched in my mind. Walter and I still talk about it.

During a bluefish blitz at Wasque one year, Walter landed a nine pound Atlantic Salmon that he threw in his cooler along with a couple of bluefish. We found out later that Atlantic Salmon were on the threatened species list and illegal to keep. Walter said "it was delicious!"

To earn gas money in the spring when the bluefishing was at its best, the four would fish commercially from the surf. The day would normally start at Wasque Point. If the Rip didn't produce, they would move, usually in a convoy to Leland's, the Snow Fence, Dike Bridge, Arruda's, the Jetties, the Elbow, and all the way to the Gut with stops along the way at Shear Pen Pond as well as the Cape Poge lighthouse. Many times, one or all of them would repeat the stops on the return trip, or if fish were breaking somewhere stop until they filled their totes at which time they would gut and ice the fish before ending their trip. On his way to his home in West Tisbury Don would sell them at Net Result in Vineyard Haven.

During the Derby there was competition among the four but unlike many cases today, it was always good natured. The fiercest competition was between Don and Gordon and many times during the Derby it was for the Senior Grand Award for bluefish. But it was usually Gordon that took home the prize as he would sneak out early in pre-dawn hours and dunk bait which was something Don absolutely detested and would never even consider. He said it was cheating and would tell Gordon that "even a blind squirrel finds an acorn once in a while!"

⚬⚬⚬

Marsh Bryan was generous to a fault. He would usually arrive on the Island in early May, spend a couple of months at his house overlooking the Bay, leave for the summer, and then return in the fall for the Derby. During the months he was gone, he would offer the house to Don and Marian and for weeks at a time they would use it as their summer get-a-way from the hustle and bustle of the tourist season on the main island. Before we moved to the Vineyard, Barbara and I would often join them for a long weekend and stay in the upper level front room, with that wonderful sweeping view of Katama Bay and South Beach.

Marsh owned a number of Ray Ellis Derby prints including the inaugural print of surfcasters at Wasque. I always loved that print as the colors and the scene itself perfectly captured the essence of the place. Even the bend in the rods and angle of the line was right. Over the years I had made some inquiries about buying one but no one wanted to part with theirs. When I finally found someone willing to sell they wanted more than $5,000 for it, which was a little rich for my blood. But for some reason Marsh never liked it. One year with my birthday fast approaching and unbeknownst to me, Barbara asked him if he would be willing to sell it. He gave it to her!!! It's number 100/100 and signed in two places by Mr. Ellis. With Wasque Point as we knew it gone, along with many of my old friends, that print holds a very special place in my heart.

Marsh was also the unofficial captain of the Viagra Fishing Team. Before the advent of cell phones iPads and text messages, the only way to communicate with other anglers on Chappy was by Citizens Band or "CB" radios. Communications were spotty at best as the range was only a mile or two and depended upon the type of day or where you were on the beach. Reception and range were better if the sky was cloudy but if the day was clear, the "skip" would sometimes carry the signal off into space. Everyone had a nickname or "handle" and was creative in their choice of names. Marsh took Redfin as his handle and was very precise and followed proper radio etiquette when communicating on the CB. When you called for the Redfin to "come in" it didn't matter who was calling or whether he recognized the voice or not, the clipped reply in his rich baritone voice would always be "this is the **Red fin**!" The only thing I can compare it to is the old Rhoda TV show staring Valerie Harper when the doorman would always answer the intercom buzzer with **"This is Carlton the Doorman."** When the conversation was over Marsh would sign off with "this is the Redfin, over and out on channel 11."

Others took on handles that either fit their persona or identified with something in their life. Walter Lison called himself the Sea Urchin. His boat carried the same name. Joe Gubitose built custom rods and was Custom Joe. Pete Conley was Poacher but I never asked about that one! Bob Clay of the Clay Family car dealerships was Empty Pockets, Fran Clay put a hook in her hand one day and became known as Bloody Hand. The Trustees night ranger Bob Ozcyz was Chow Hound. Gordon Ditchfield was the Englishman and Don Mohr could be no one else but Coach. There were others like the Polish Prince (Charlie Stula), Mad Dog (Mark Carlson), Hammer (me). Dan Geary was Echo and always used a descending tone to sound like a real echo. Charlie Barr was Beer Man, and Abe Williams was Honest Abe. It was fun!

One year Marsh established a rather simple numbered code system to identify all of the fishing spots on Chappy and gave everyone a handwritten sheet with all the codes. Wasque was #1, Lelands #2 all the way to the Gut which was #11. He shared it with the Viagra Fishing Team as well as others in his circle of fishing buddies and we used it to communicate and share fishing reports as we ran the beaches. If I remember right, the channel used for normal communications was 19 but for our 'secret' system we used channel 11. To some extent, and for a short period of time, it worked well until someone accidently found us. We switched channels for awhile but by then guys were on to us and we could easily be found by anyone intent on finding us.

When we first started using the system the conversation would often go something like this. "Echo, this is the Hammer, you out there?" Echo would respond with "how you *doin, doin, doin, doin, doin?*" "Good, I'm just leaving #3 and there's nothing going on here." Echo would respond with something like, "gotcha, I'm at #7 and think I saw a swirl!" If one or more of the team was listening, they would join the conversation with "hey, Hammer and Echo, this is the Sea Urchin, I'm at #10 and there are some bluefish here." Where upon everyone would look at their chart to see where #10 was and move there. But no one memorized the numbers and after a week or two we tired of the secrecy and hassle of looking at the chart and the conversation went more like this. "Echo, this is the Hammer, how you *doin, doin, doin, doin, doin?*" *"Fine, fine, fine, fine. Fine,"* came the reply. "Dan, I'm just leaving Wasque, where you at?" "I'm at Arruda's and there are some fish busting here" and anyone listening on channel 11 ended up at Arruda's or followed the convoy racing in that direction.

To get to Marsh's house on Chappaquiddick you were required to take a turn off the paved main road onto unpaved Litchfield Road, take another turn onto a dirt road, drive past a few homes some of which were occupied year round, through a salt marsh, up a precarious drive on the edge of a bluff overlooking the marsh, crest the hill, and make a quick left turn into the driveway at the rear of his house.

It wasn't until you entered the place that you got a full appreciation for its setting. As you came in through the back door, your eyes were immediately drawn to the million dollar view out front. There was a small kitchen to the right and a hallway to the left took you to the master bedroom which also had an ocean view. But as you continued toward the front you entered a huge great room with a beautiful fieldstone fireplace on the left and a dining area on the right. A couch faced the fireplace and behind the couch were Marsh's rod building table and work bench. The front entrance was ahead and exited onto a beautiful patio with a panoramic view of the bay and front beach. At the base of the hill was a small salt pond that drained into Katama Bay.

Dan and Versie Geary are retirees from Meriden, CT and were caretakers of Marsh's house and they are also avid Derby anglers. Before they retired to Chappaquiddick in 1990, every morning for more than thirty years, Dan drove a truck delivering bottled milk to homes in the Meriden area.

In 2002 using an old 2 oz. Atom Popper with faded colors and rusted hooks that he had resurrected from Marsh's garage, Dan made three casts one afternoon and caught a 15.69 lb. bluefish that ended up as the Shore Bluefish Grand Leader with a shot at the Grand Prize Boston Whaler. He didn't win the boat that year but walked away with more than $3,000 in prizes as well as numerous senior awards. Though he was disappointed that he didn't win the Grand Prize, the most important thing to him was the fact that he had achieved a certain level of immortality as his name will appear forever in the annual Derby program. He is also justifiably proud that there hasn't been a bigger shore Grand Leader bluefish since!

Dan and Versie would also occasionally score Derby pins with striped bass and no one could figure out where they were catching them as neither were hard core striper anglers and neither fished at night. But somehow, through loose lips or the process of elimination, word got out that they were fishing right below Marsh's house, and in broad daylight.

Very early one morning I had run the front beach to catch the end of a tide at the hard, or North Neck side of the Cape Poge Gut. My plan was to fish the predawn hours for bass and be there at first light for the albie bite. The bass bite never materialized but I did catch a small albie before the tide ended and the morning crowd started to arrive. During the Derby every morning at around 7:15 AM and for an hour or so after, a steady procession of anglers arrives at the Gut as the three-car On Time Ferry starts running from Edgartown. You can almost set your watch by it. Consequently, it can get very crowded as it's easy to access and albies crash bait, sometimes almost at your feet. It's a mecca for fly fishermen.

I decided to look for greener albie pastures on East Beach but as I was coming out of North Neck Road that precise baritone voice crackled on the CB. "Hammer, this is the Redfin calling on channel 11-over!" "Hi Marsh, what's up?" "Hammer, we're at my house and there are stripers out front-over." "10-4 Marsh, I'm just coming out of North Neck, I'll be there in a few minutes."

It was a short drive and I made it even shorter by driving as fast as I possibly could. When I crested the hill and turned into Marsh's circular driveway, it looked like Wasque Point on a sunny day in May. Everyone in our small gang was there and Marsh was hanging out with a coffee and a cigarette. "They're down in front and hitting poppers," he said. I grabbed my ten-footer, a couple of poppers and a yellow bomber and about sprinted the fifty yards down the tick infested hill to the bottom.

Bob Clay was there as well as Bob Ozcyz, Don Mohr, Gordon Ditchfield, Walter Lison, and Dan and Versie. I didn't see any fish on the beach but my first cast into the flat calm shallow water brought an explosion on my Super Strike popper. Hoots and hollers erupted when I missed the fish but the next cast produced the same result only this time I landed a fish in the mid-teens.

A few more fish were caught before the action ended and I learned that it had been going on since first light and most of the fish were in the twelve to fifteen pound range. With the exception of Don, who had driven down, we all hiked our way up the hill to the back of the house where Marsh was waiting. I had to use the bathroom and started to take my waders off but Marsh said not to worry about it, just go right in. I had to go badly but the thought of scraping up that beautiful hardwood floor with wet sand still on my boots just blew my mind so off they came in a hurry.

We fished there every morning for the rest of the week until the action slowed then finally died completely. But we had found a new spot, simply called Marsh's House and for the next few years used it as our unofficial clubhouse. As always Marsh was the perfect host providing a hot cup of coffee and a clean toilet facility.

In 2004, for reasons we'll probably never know, Marsh announced to us that he was putting the house up for sale. It didn't take long for it to sell and we learned it was sold to his next door neighbor who tore it down and built a mega-mansion very similar to the one he already owned. Marsh said later that if he had known it was going to be demolished he never would have sold it. He was very angry with the agent.

We haven't seen him since he sold the house and to the best of our knowledge he has not been back to the Island. The last we heard, he and Helen were Master Bridge players and competing on a regular basis. A couple of years after he left the island, he called Don Mohr and told him he was giving away most of his fishing gear and wanted Don and me to have first dibs. Don and Marian visited the Bryans at their house in New Jersey and returned with three Van Staal reels, rods, most of them wrapped by Marsh himself, a number of other reels, hundreds of lures, and miscellaneous fishing gear. Don kept a Van Staal 200 and a 150 and I accepted a gift of a Van Staal 200 and a custom built Marsh Bryan rod. The rest of the tackle was distributed to Marsh's friends on Chappy, donated to a special needs individual and the high school fishing club.

We kept in touch for a while and exchanged cards at Christmas time but as things go sometimes, we have lost touch. As for the remainder of the Viagra Fishing Team, Gordon Ditchfield died of cancer in 1999 and Don passed away in 2012. Walter Lison still lives on the Vineyard but is in his 80's with bad knees and doesn't fish much anymore.

ABE WILLIAMS

Barbara and I moved permanently to the Vineyard in 2002 and during the June new moon that year, the striper fishing on Chappy was outstanding. Word got out in a hurry and every night for a week the quarter mile stretch of beach from the jetties to the Cape Poge lighthouse was lined with anywhere from seventy five to a hundred anglers, and everyone caught fish that weighed up to thirty pounds.

A bunch of us would arrive early and try to stake out a piece of beach just below the bluff on the east side of the lighthouse, and besides being what we thought was the most productive spot, we could look south and see what was happening all the way to the jetties. Once it got good and dark, head and neck lights would start flickering up and down the beach as anglers unhooked fish. There were so many lights on at times, it looked like candles being held at a memorial service. It really didn't matter what lure or fly you used because just about everything worked, but Abe Williams and I were

THREE DECADES OF THE DERBY

having very good luck with black 2 oz. Danny's, until the third night when I had an unfortunate mishap.

I was unhooking a fish when it flipped and put one of the trebles into the fleshy part of the palm on my left hand just below my thumb. Abe was right there to help me subdue the fish and get it off the lure, but with the 3/0 hook buried in my hand well past the barb and no wire cutter available, it was obvious I was going to the emergency room. Abe and Bob Clay helped me get my waders off and my rod loaded on the roof rack and with the Danny still attached I was off down the beach then the main road to the Chappy Ferry. And finally, the fifteen minute ride to the hospital in Vineyard Haven. It killed me to leave such good fishing.

During the course of a year the emergency room staff at the Vineyard Hospital sees a lot of embedded hooks and is very adept at removing them. Although the resident said he was from Vermont

and more used to removing tiny trout hooks than 3/0 trebles, I was out of there in less than an hour. When I got back to the car, there was Abe, sitting in his vehicle watching over my rods. He had left some great fishing to look after a friend.

Abe and his sidekick Charlie (Beer Man) Barr were unofficial members of the Viagra

Fishing team. It was kind of a Batman, Robin relationship. Most of us thought that Abe was the best fisherman of our entire group and by association, Charlie was too.

Abe was a thin man of average height with about the whitest hair and beard I ever saw. If he had lived in another time, he would have fit right in wearing a robe and sandals and carrying a Shepard's staff rather than a fishing pole. He smoked heavily and always wore a blue Derby hat tilted slightly back on his head. When you talked with Abe on the beach you always had his attention but rarely did he look you directly in the eyes. This was not because he was shy or self-conscious, instead his gaze was usually focused on the water.

Charlie was a Korean War vet and a good guy but as his CB handle Beer Man might suggest, was the opposite of Abe. Abe was on the quiet side, while Charlie was full of bluster. Abe was low key and would rarely share fishing stories while Charlie would freely tell you about every fish he caught and to prove how good he was would line the dashboard of his car with big wooden lures. It was a work of art! About the only thing they appeared  to have in common was their love for the sport and their beach buggies. Both drove older vehicles at the time and in different ways, nursed them until they belched their last puff of exhaust. Charlie went a step further. When I first met him he was driving an old 70's vintage Jeep Cherokee with a floor so rusted out that when his wife Tina joined him for an afternoon on the beach, she was forced to sit on an old plastic milk crate because the passenger seat had rusted right off the floor.

My first encounter with Abe took place one Memorial Day weekend in the mid eighties at Wasque Point. He was there with all five of his sons, Abe Jr., Dan, Greg, Dennis and Doug as well as his partner Maryann Henninger. They arrived in an old blue Chevy Suburban and when they piled out of the vehicle and unloaded all of their gear and coolers, it was like watching fifteen people get out of a clown car at a circus.

They were a hard partying group of guys having some family fun and if it wasn't already a normal zoo at Wasque during one of the busiest weekends of the year, their gang of seven made it even worse. The annual Martha's Vineyard Rod & Gun Club Memorial Day Bluefish Tournament was going on and that event usually brought out just about every local and visiting surf angler on the island. Between the Williams gang, the Twin Tower Bergeron brothers and all the drinking and ya-hooing going on, plus tangled lines and lost fish, it was almost unpleasant to fish there. You certainly had reason to question your sanity but the prospect of catching bluefish after bluefish until your arms got sore kept everyone in the game. Needless to say, the Williams gang was not a popular group.

The annual Rod & Gun Club Memorial Day event was always a big deal and a fun event to enter. There were many entrants and a lot of prizes including nice cash awards for the winners and of course the always important 'braggin rights.' One year Abe and the boys showed up five minutes after the close of the three-day event with big bluefish that would have taken first and second place. When I asked Dan about it he told me that they had been drinking beer and catching bluefish at the Cape Poge jetties. He said both were good and they kept delaying their trip to the Gun Club weigh-in. "Dad had a two piece rod and it started to separate. When he hooked up on another blue it snapped in half. After that, we thought we had better get to the weigh-in. Dad was driving but got lost trying to find the Gun Club. It was after that tournament that we made a decision to fish or drink beer, but not both at the same time."

As the years progressed and striper stocks recovered, the Williams gang, like the rest of us, discovered there was another world beyond Wasque that also included stripers, bonito and false albacore. Abe and the boys became hardcore fishermen. Arguably, Abe was the best out there. He possessed great instincts and never impatiently jumped from spot to spot like many of us did back then. If the fish weren't there when he arrived, he would always spend at least twenty minutes in a spot allowing time for fish to move through. It's advice I still try to follow today.

At age sixty and in spite of his smoking, Abe possessed the same energy as his younger sons. When the tide was right during the Derby, he would make an almost daily forty minute trek up the front beach of Squibnocket with one or more of his sons. Anyone who knows that beach knows it is an arduous and dangerous walk over at least a mile of bowling ball size rocks that has twisted more than a few ankles and broken a couple of legs. Very often he would make the return trip with a bass slung over his shoulder. He would then drive down island, weigh the fish and head to Chappy where he would stand on the jetties or head to the Gut making the requisite thousand casts for one or two albies. Finally, around noon he would head back to his house, catch a few hours of sleep and then return for the late afternoon tide at the Rip, and it would start all over again. The man never seemed to tire.

When the Derby committee put stripers back in the Derby, many of us started focusing much of our attention away from blues and tuna like fish to striped bass. It was a learning curve for many of us as we had been weaned on bluefish and had to learn a new game. Sure, we caught a few stripers during daylight hours, particularly at the end of a bluefish blitz and a couple of pins were even won, but it was time to become striper fisherman.

Abe learned in a hurry that the way to catch stripers was to burn the midnight oil. I wasn't far behind but still confined most of my striper excursions to the beaches of Chappy so I could fish the early morning tides for albies, bonito and blues. Abe, on the other hand, searched out new locations on other parts of the island. He and his sons were fishing places like Squibby, Cedar Tree Neck, Makoniky, and other undisclosed locations, and they scored Derby pins on a regular basis. Many nights, they would fish up island spots, make the drive back down island, run the front beach to Chappy to fish the dropping tide at the Rip, and then make their way to the Gut via the jetties, the Cape Poge lighthouse and the Windmill.

As we made the transition to striper fishing, Abe was one of the few guys I could count on seeing on the Chappy beaches at all hours of the night and I always looked forward to running into him. Early one morning on a moonless, flat calm and quiet night I was on the soft side of the Gut drifting eels on an incoming tide, and with the exception of some small fish chasing bait on the other side, you could almost hear a pin drop. There wasn't a soul around me and I was having a pretty good night.

When you fish the soft side of the Gut at night, you can look east across Pocha Pond and easily see vehicle headlights traveling north along the inner trail toward the Cape Poge Lighthouse. Also, if a vehicle approaches the Gut from the north, its headlights signal its approach by illuminating the bluffs on the North Neck side. I had been there for about an hour and with the exception of a couple of chunkers on South Beach hadn't passed a soul on the long drive out from Katama. I also had not seen any headlights to the east and none coming toward the Gut from the north.

Suddenly, I was aware of movement and some noise behind me and it about scared me out of my waders. I turned around to see a black vehicle without lights of any kind approaching very slowly from the north. It came around the bend, crept behind me and stopped at the western end of the small beach. Quietly, and without a word, five guys bailed out of a black Blazer and started throwing eels. It was Abe and the boys!

If you are a striper fisherman, you know the unmistakable sound of an eel being cast. It's a unique sound and a little hard to describe but to me it sounds something like a World War ll artillery shell in flight. For those of you that have never heard it, it's kind of a *'whir-ring- whistling'* sound and for the next half hour there was a constant artillery barrage as eels were repeatedly being cast, retrieved and cast again. All this time, hardly a word was spoken as the boys moved up and down the beach, always keeping a respectable distance from where I was fishing. None of us hooked up and almost as quietly as they came, they got back in the vehicle and left. It wasn't until they were well around the bend that they turned their headlights on as they made their way north toward the Windmill House and out of there.

One year, Abe and the boys were scoring striper pins on a daily basis but as usual were closed mouth about the whole thing. With one day left in the Derby, Abe quietly confided to me that for the last week they had been scoring a lot of fish up to twenty five pounds by throwing eels at a spot about a forty minute walk from the parking lot at Squibby. He said he was tired and based on the size of the fish they had been catching didn't think they had any chance of making the leader board which was led by Mark Plante's forty seven pound fish, so he was not going up there again.

My friend Ernie Baracchini and I were unfazed by this and buoyed by the report decided to make the long dangerous trek up the rocky beach. We arrived around 3:00 AM, about two hours into the rising tide, and after a half hour of searching, found some fish more than willing to eat our eels. The fish were in the fifteen to twenty pound range, there were a lot of them and they were hungry.

We only had a dozen eels between us and it soon became apparent that they were not going to last long. Almost every cast produced a pick up or a fish and as the morning marched toward dawn, some bigger fish moved in and our fifteen to twenty pound fish became twenty five to thirty pounders. We were having a ball but releasing everything as we were hoping for a fish that would get us on the leader board. Every cast seemed to produce a bigger fish than the last.

I was down to my last eel and it was starting to get a little light when I landed a fish in the low thirties. I briefly gave some thought to keeping it for at least a daily pin, but I was certain there was a bigger one out there and couldn't get the fish or myself back in the water fast enough. I waded back out, made a cast and as soon as my eel hit the water a big fish inhaled the eel. The circle hook did its thing and after one very long run I was able to work it through the boulders and onto the rocky beach.

The fish was big and had a huge head. I called Ernie over to look at it and he said, "buddy, I think you have the grand *pooh bah* there!" It was a good fish but I didn't think it was big enough to win the whole thing. I decided to weigh it anyway thinking it might be a top three fish or at the very least a weekly winner. It was the last night of the Derby and had been a very slow week with no fish over thirty pounds weighed in. We fished for a while longer and Ernie landed a fish in the high twenties that he kept but we ran out of eels and the fish did not seem to have the same interest in our Sluggos. It was also getting pretty light.

When it came time to leave, I realized that I had forgotten my drag rope. Fortunately, Ernie had the forethought to bring a burlap bag with a rope tie on it so we loaded the sixty-plus pounds of fish in it, each took an end, and off we went on the death march back to the parking lot.

It was one of those mild and slightly humid late fall days and we soon realized that it was going to take a very long time to get back to our vehicles if we continued along the front beach. In addition, dragging more than sixty pounds of fish behind us along with all our gear was wearing us out so we made the decision to climb the bluff and drag ourselves and the fish down the main road back to our vehicles.

As we were approaching the top of a short hill, Ernie stopped me and said, "dude, look up ahead." I was hot and soaking wet from sweat and my glasses were so fogged I couldn't see a thing. Thinking we were outed, I asked what was there. "The biggest buck you'll ever see," but by the time I put my gear down and got my glasses cleaned off, the deer was gone.

As we crested the hill, we still had more than a mile to go and I was totally exhausted. It was the last night of a Derby that I had fished hard and I had had it! I stopped Ernie and said something like, why don't you stay here with the fish and the gear, and I'll go get the car, drive back and pick you up. If anyone sees you and complains, just start limping and tell them you sprained your ankle and I went to get the car. He wasn't crazy about the idea but reluctantly agreed.

The sun was full up by the time I got back to the parking area. There were a lot of cars there and a number of guys were standing around talking. I avoided the stares, got into my vehicle and drove the mile to where Ernie was waiting. We quickly loaded the fish and gear into the car and out we went. Nobody stopped us and nobody in the parking lot questioned us. The ruse had worked and we agreed to meet at the weigh station a few hours later.

My fish weighed thirty five pounds and Ernie's, twenty seven. Surprisingly, someone had walked in a half hour earlier with a fish in the low forties. After all that work and deception, I not only didn't make it onto the overall leader board, I didn't win the weekly prize or even a daily gold pin. My fish ended up as a daily second and Ernie's took third. That fish remains the biggest Derby striper I ever weighed.

In 1996, Abe's son Dennis was a Derby Grand Leader for catching the largest shore bluefish. The fish weighed 18.47 lbs. and no one knows where he caught it.

A couple of years later in 1998, Abe and Dennis were fishing eels and bailing on bass to fifteen pounds. Abe said later there were so many fish it actually got boring. On one cast, he had a pick-up, hooked the fish, turned his back to it, put the rod over his shoulder like he was carrying a sack of potatoes, and started to walk away from the water saying "oh well, I got another one." The bass turned out to be a 20.58 lb. bluefish that ran down the beach toward Dennis. As Abe caught up to it and hauled the fish on the beach, Dennis saw what it was and pinned the giant bluefish to the sand by throwing his entire body on it. Of course the fish was the Grand Leader in the Shore Bluefish Division and Abe later said, "Ignorance is bliss."

To this day the location of the place he caught it remains a closely guarded family secret and in the eighteen years since Dennis and Abe caught their fish, only two shore bluefish weighing more than eighteen pounds have been weighed in, and no one from either the boat or shore division has weighed in a twenty pounder.

Abe and I shared a mutual goal of winning the Grand Slam and had a few late night discussions about why the Derby does not award a Grand Prize key to the winners of the division. Anyone entered in the Derby can make that one lucky cast and catch the largest of one of the four eligible species giving them a one in four chance to win the Grand Prize boat or truck, but it takes an incredible combination of hard work, luck and skill to win the Grand Slam. We agreed that the Grand Slam winners are the best fishermen on the island during the five week event and should have at least the same consideration.

2002 was the first year I could fish the entire five weeks of the Derby. Unlike years gone by when you could almost always count on catching a bonito if you put in the time and made the requisite 5,000 casts, catching one these days is like finding a proverbial needle in a hay stack and only a handful are caught by shore anglers each year.

During the first week of the 2002 event I was lucky enough to catch one at the Rip. Around the same time Abe caught one on Chappy Beach and the race was on to see which of us was going to win the Grand Slam. For me, the striper came next, then the albie and all that was left was a bluefish. Abe took a similar route with an albie, then a striper.

We were in, as all we had to do was catch a 22" bluefish - a *22" bluefish*, how hard could that be? Ha, little did we know what a difficult task it was going to be. We both expected it to happen within a day or two but it didn't! One day dragged into the next - Wasque, the Jetties, Shear Pen Pond, the Gut. Plenty of bluefish but not one over 22". Every day Abe and I would check with each other to see if the other guy had caught the Derby legal bluefish and every day we would laugh about the fact that it hadn't happened. But it was killing me and I was telling my tale of woe to everyone that would listen. I was embarrassed that I couldn't catch a lousy 22" bluefish and I made a fool out of myself for whining about it.

Days dragged into weeks and I was chasing bluefish reports all over the island as the daily pin winners were pretty good size fish. One day, although I was sworn to secrecy, I got a report of nine to ten pound bluefish being caught with eels at a spot along the north shore that I had never fished before. I scouted it out by walking the mile long trail through thick woods and down a steep hill. It looked very fishy and I decided I would fish it early the next morning.

When I got up at 2:00 AM, the wind was howling out of the southeast and it was raining hard. Undaunted, I headed for the spot and started the walk. It was pitch black and wet and I thought to myself, this is absolutely insane. If my light ever fails or if I venture off the trail or fall, I'm going to be in serious trouble until daylight. Fortunately, that didn't happen and I finally got to the spot but all I caught was two more undersize bluefish and a small striper.

Abe was doing similar things and all the while we were adding to our total weight by catching larger striped bass. Between us, Abe had the overall lead. At first light one morning, I was dunking bait out in front of Dike Bridge when I caught a bluefish that measured 22 ¼" on my tape and just over 22" lying flat on my Igloo cooler. George Moran was there and he got the same measurement. This was it, I got it! Even if I didn't win or finish in the top three of the

Grand Slam Division, I had finally achieved my goal and at the very least would get my coveted Grand Slam pin.

I threw the fish in the cooler and raced off to the weigh-in. It was embarrassing just to walk in the door with a bluefish that small and even more embarrassing when they put the fish on the measuring board and it was short by a quarter of an inch. I was devastated!

I never got my bluefish that year and I still think about it. Abe finally got his just a few days before the Derby ended and his fish was just over the 22' minimum. Needless to say, his total weight was not enough to get him a top three finish but at least he got his Grand Slam pin. It came without any fanfare but I ate my heart out when Derby President Ed Jerome handed it to him at the Awards Ceremony.

One night in June of 2003, Abe and I were hunting bass together at Arruda Point on Chappy but all we were catching were bluefish in the 8-10 lb. range. As the night wore on, we expected the bluefish to go to bed and stripers to arrive and every time we hooked a fish that pulled some drag, we would optimistically remark that it felt like a bass. Finally, Abe hooked something that really started pulling line. "Here we go" he said and took off down the beach after the fish. He was gone quite a while and I fully expected him to be carrying a big striper when he returned, but the bass we had been hoping for turned out to be a foul hooked nine pound bluefish.

I finally gave up and went home around midnight but Abe said he was going to hang in awhile longer. The next morning, his good friend Charlie couldn't get in touch with him and later found him at home, dead on his couch.

I learned just recently from Mark Wrabel that bass showed up in force shortly after I left.

Maryann Henninger and Abe's family asked that memorial donations be made to the Martha's Vineyard Striped Bass and Bluefish Derby or the Martha's Vineyard Surfcasters Association. They also established a Derby award to be given to the angler who is first to achieve a Grand Slam every year. When I finally achieved my Grand Slam a few years ago, I missed winning the Abe Williams Memorial Award by just a few hours to my young friend, and outstanding surf angler, Julian Pepper.

A few years later Abe's son Greg caught a bonito, then a striper, and later an albie. He was in position to win his Dad's award, but as luck would have it, couldn't catch a bluefish. At the same time, Chappy regular and friend Phil Horton had also caught the elusive bonito, a bluefish and albie but not a Derby legal 32'" striper.

In a true display of Derby sportsmanship, Phil, being the good guy that he is, wanted Greg to win his Dad's award and vowed not to weigh in a striper before Greg weighed in his bluefish. Early one morning Greg got a cell phone call from Phil informing him that he had caught his striper but if Greg had caught his bluefish he was willing to wait until after Greg weighed it. That turned out not to be the case and Greg told Phil to go ahead and weigh it in so someone we all knew would win.

Greg eventually caught his bluefish and went on to win the Grand Slam that year. Phil won the Abe Williams Award.

In 2012 the Derby Committee saw fit to give Phil the Martha's Vineyard Surfcasters Sportsmanship Award. What goes round comes around!

In the ten years since he passed away, the Abe Williams Award has also been won by Jack Livingston, Keith McArt, and Dave Balon, all Abe's friends from Chappy.

The Martha's Vineyard Surfcasters established the Abe Williams Memorial annual award for the member who catches the largest shore striped bass every year. I'm proud and honored to say that I won it the first year and again a few years later. Also, at Maryann and the boys' request, the Surfcasters placed a memorial bench on the beautiful overlook at the Cape Poge Lighthouse. If you are out that way and never been there, take a walk out, the view is stunning. The memorial plaque reads, *"In Memory of Abe Williams, Always Watching the Water."*

Of his five sons, only Dan and Greg carry on Abe's legacy. Both are hard core anglers and consistent pin winners. In addition to his Grand Slam win, Greg also finished third in the same category a few years later and along with Dan's son-in-law Brad Johnston, seem to be the only ones who can pull a rabbit out of a hat almost every year by catching a rare Chappy bonito. But there will never be another Abe Williams!

AL ANGELONE

THE SECOND PERSON that fits my description of one of the most unforgettable characters I ever met is Al Angelone and I couldn't write a book about island surfcasters and the Derby without writing a chapter about 'Angie'. Although I only knew the man for four short years he was a very special person and in the seventy plus years I've been on this planet, he touched my life in a way not many other people have.

The first time I met Angie, or Ang, was on South Beach in the spring of 2002, the year we moved to the Vineyard. I was fishing for schoolies when this burly, muscular looking guy comes walking over and starts talking to me like we were best friends. I was a little taken aback by it at first but after a few minutes found myself liking the guy and amused by his personality and mannerisms. He was smoking a pipe and wearing a faded and well worn gray University of Tennessee baseball cap with the trademark orange 'T' on it. It looked like it had been around forever.

He was a little on the short side, looked to be in his early to mid sixties and talked with a heavy New York accent. The first words out of his mouth were "how ya doin" which I soon learned was his standard greeting and one that I would hear often over the next few years. We talked mainly about fishing but when we got around to talking about ourselves and he learned I was born and raised in New Britain, CT, *(New Britnn if you were born there)* he really got cranked up. He knew all about it as he had coached the wrestling team at the University of Hartford where he had earned his Master's Degree after a stint in the Marine Corps. He told me he was born on Long Island in the town of Rockaway Beach and I learned later he received his Bachelor's Degree from Adelphi University in Garden City, NY where he excelled at lacrosse and wrestling. *(Ang is a member of the Adelphi Sports Hall of Fame.)*

Over the summer I would occasionally run into him at Dog Fish Bar where he would fish with his wife Mary Ann. The ever present pipe would be hanging from one side of his mouth and he would talk out of the other side or remove the pipe and use it to emphasize a point. He was very animated and talked a lot with his hands and to be sure you got the message, would always ask, "ya know what I mean?" But as Nelson Sigelman, the Editor and author of the weekly 'Gone Fishin' column for The Martha's Vineyard Times said, "more often than not, I didn't know what he meant." He was one dedicated fisherman and all business when he was on the beach, but if you saw him in town the next day, he would gladly discuss the previous night's fishing.

Unlike today, in the late 90's and into the mid 2000's the late spring fishing at Lobsterville and Dogfish Bar was an outstanding flyrod and light tackle fishery, and the stretch from the Menemsha Jetty west toward Gay Head was usually loaded with sand eels and hungry stripers. Almost every night Ang and Mary Ann would arrive early at Dogfish Bar and stake out a spot along the beach where they would throw a special Ang modified 1 oz. light green Spofford's Needlefish at fish that would sometimes be so close you had to back up and cast almost parallel to the beach. Everyone, including Ang and Mary Ann, would have a ball. Most of the fish were schoolie size up to 35" but on occasion during the course of a night some bigger fish would move through and fish up to 30 lbs. would be caught. Ang and Mary Ann landed their share of them and if they hooked a fish that made a long run and put the light tackle to the test, Ang liked to say it "took off to Hyannis."

During the Derby that year I saw more of them as they would often fish East Beach on Chappy, primarily the area in front of Dike Bridge which is a consistent spot for catching false albacore and an occasional bonito. While the rest of us chased pods of false albacore up and down the beach, Ang and Mary Ann would stay put for hours in the same spot. I would always stop to say hello but as was usually the case when he fished all I got was a quick hello or a nod of the head as they continually cast their needlefish. As always Ang had the ever present pipe in his mouth and Tennessee baseball cap on his head. I got out of the car once to take a picture of the two of them but Ang stopped me saying, "no pictures, no pictures."

In the off season that year, I got to know Ang a little better and enjoyed running into him at the post office or church on Sunday (he loved the children's mass), and during visits to Larry's Tackle Shop where I worked. I even ran into him at the Martha's Vineyard Hospital one day and he seemed to know everyone there.

Everybody loved the guy. He had a great sense of humor and that New York accent of his, as well as his way of using his hands and pipe to drive home a point, made him a very funny guy. He also spouted plenty of 'Angisms'. I once told him I knew someone that lived in a beach front co-op at Breezy Point in the Rockaway's and he said he knew exactly where it was. He had dated a girl in high school and they used to go *"smoochin"* under a boardwalk light there. He laughed all the way thru the story.

On another occasion we were talking college basketball and he re- marked about the rivalry between the UConn and Tennessee wom- en's basketball teams. I've been a fan of the UConn men's basketball team for as long as I can remember and I said something like "I like the men." Ang found a lot of humor in that statement and joked about it often over the next few years.

Three or four times a year they breach the Tisbury Pond as they do to most of the larger coastal ponds along the south shore. The intent is to keep the salinity level high and the shellfish healthy. When they do this the fishing is usually pretty good as the outflow acts like a giant chum slick releasing anything trapped in the pond since the previous opening.

After a few days of the tide carrying the outflow scent up and down the beach, any stripers within range of the opening seem to gravitate to the area. The spring fishing is usually pretty consistent as it often coincides with the arrival of herring. It provides anglers who have been waiting all winter long a good opportunity to put a bend in a rod. The timing was good when they breached Tisbury that spring as it was right around the time some bigger fish were arriving and it provided some pretty good day time fishing.

I met Ang in town one day and mentioned it to him. To my surprise, he told me he had never fished there as the walk to the opening was a long 'hump' from Quansoo. I told him there was another way in from Long Point and that the walk from the parking lot was an easy one over hard packed dirt and firm sand along the edge of the pond. He seemed interested but hesitant and I told him I would call him before I went the next time. A day or two later I called and he agreed to join me. I picked him up at his house and we had a pretty fair afternoon. I learned a little more about him when he told me he spent his career working for the Secret Service. When I asked what branch, all he would reveal was the counterfeiting division. Later when I dropped him off at his house he asked me to come in but I politely declined. The next day he showed up at Larry's, took me outside and handed me a dark blue coffee mug with the Secret Service logo emblazoned in gold on it. He said, "they don't sell these, so be careful with it."

We fished together a number of times over the next few years and often made the 'hump' to the opening as well as fished for bluefish at the Wasque Rip. As was often the case in the late spring the Rip was inaccessible to ORV's because of nesting Piping Plovers so we were forced to park in the Fishermen's Parking lot, take the stairs down along the edge of the bluffs and walk the boardwalk to the beach.

Most of the time we fished the Rip we would meet at Larry's and he would drive, but when we fished the Tisbury opening, I would pick him up on the way to Long Point. Every time I dropped him off at his house he would ask me to come in, but there always seemed to be somewhere else I had to be, or something else I had to do, so I never went in.

———✦———

The year before I met Ang in 2001, he took second place in the coveted Shore Grand Slam Division and I learned that he loved to fish for bonito. He would start looking for the first bonito in early August, sometimes even late July at places they usually show up first like the Big Bridge or Tashmoo.

Late one Saturday morning in July I walked into Larry's and Steve Purcell asked me if I had seen Ang. He told me that Mary Ann had called and said Angie was late to return home from an early morning fishing trip and she was concerned. He said she asked that if we were on the beach could we please keep an eye out for him. A bad feeling washed over me. I ran the beach at Norton Point and called my friends on Chappy and asked if anyone had seen him. No one had. Anglers all over the island were looking for him.

Early that evening his friends Cooper Gilkes and Robbie Morrison went to a spot near Mink Meadows and found him on the sand. As Nelson Sigelman said in his column "there is no sadness that he died on an island he loved doing what he loved." Mary Ann told Nelson, "Island fishermen are the greatest people in the world."

Nelson wrote about Ang In his weekly 'Gone Fishin' column for the Times. He said he knew him as "kind of a quirky, friendly guy who loved to fish, often alone and at odd hours of the day" and that "he was a hard fisherman on an Island of hard fishermen."

While preparing for the article, he talked to George Rogers, the Secret Service's Assistant Director of the Office of Inspection. George told him he was from upstate New York and liked to hunt and fish. When Ang learned George liked to fish he assured him that despite the fact they were in the heart of New York City they could still catch fish and they agreed to meet at 5:00 AM one morning near their office where the World Trade Center used to stand. From there they drove to Kennedy airport and parked. He said: "we walked out past weeds, willows, junk refrigerators, and broken down rusty cars and ended up fishing right off the approach of some runway. It must have been about every six minutes one of these jets would come over, but you know what? We caught fish."

Nelson also learned that Ang joined the Secret Service in 1968 and was assigned to the New York field office but his toughness and street smarts soon earned him a transfer to the New York special detail as a key member of an undercover team tracking down counterfeiters. On one assignment he went undercover in a jail cell. During the incarceration, one of his cellmates noticed Ang was wearing shoes while the rest of them were wearing standard issue inmate slippers. When he questioned Ang about it, he replied, "I got no toes!"

Ang was later transferred to the presidential protection division and director Rogers said some people questioned the wisdom of transferring such a street wise agent to the more visible post. But Nelson spoke with Ang's close friend and former agent Frank Forgione of Edgartown who described him as a 'force to be reckoned with'. He described the 1975 assassination attempt on President Gerald Ford when Sara Jane Moore fired one shot at the President from a 38-caliber hand gun. While everyone else was ducking or trying to push the President down, Ang stood tall near the left front fender of the Presidential limousine with his jacket open and his hand on his weapon. The scene was captured by a photographer and appeared on the front cover of Life Magazine as well as newspapers across the country. The photo now resides in the National Archives.

We had a real American hero in our midst and were clueless about it!

Stories and tributes about Angie flooded in on the funeral home web-site. Many of his former colleagues described him as a hero and more than one called him a legend in the United States Secret Service. Pat Nixon was afraid of him. He made President Carter laugh. The White House staff loved him, as much as the Secret Service detail did. One agent told a story about Ang walking in the Rose Garden with President Ford's arm over his shoulder. He said "the President stops and shoves some money in Angie's pocket, then enters the oval office. Later Angie turns to me laughing and

says," he's queer for Michigan, but he always gives too many points."
(Michigan was Ford's alma mater)

Another agent told about an incident that eventually helped end Angie's career in the Secret Service. He and Ang had been assigned to teach a group of foreign agents protective driving techniques using an armored limousine. Angie put them in the car and said not to touch anything; he would control all the doors. No sooner had he said that when one of them closed the back door and took off Angie's finger. Ang looked down, calmly picked up his finger and without any shouting or distress, turned to the agent and said: "now look what the hell you did, you cut off my finger. I'm going to get some attention and be right back." The agent fainted! They all said they were sorry and that he must be the bravest agent in the Secret Service. When Ang got to the hospital, he told the doctors that he needed his finger because he was giving a harp concert at Carnegie Hall in two weeks.

Finally, an agent wrote, "All of his Secret Service brothers and sisters have a special place in their hearts for Angie. He brought smiles to our faces and love to our hearts. As long as there is one agent alive that was touched by Angie's special manner, he will be immortal."

In addition to leaving his wife Mary Ann, Angie left two sons, Anthony, who at the time was a Marine Corps Captain serving in Malaysia after tours in Iraq and Afghanistan, and Peter, who followed in his father's footsteps and is a Secret Service agent.

In perhaps the best compliment a husband and father could receive and a testament to Angie's incredible character Mary Ann said, "he guarded presidents but the most important thing in his life was his family. He was very proud of his two sons. He always put his family first. He put them before the job, he put them before fishing, he put them before everything."

Peter Angelone said that his father, who devoted so much time to serving his country and community, always found time for his family even if it meant driving four hours each way for a twenty minute visit. "He always had the energy to come home and do simple things."

I miss Ang! We all miss him. I feel like I was building something that was stolen from me before I finished it. I regret that I didn't get to know him better and I regret that I didn't fish with him more often. I even regret not going into his house when he asked me. I think Nelson summed it up for many of us when he said: "Funny what we don't know about the people we meet. I wish now I'd spent more time talking to Angie." I still have the blue Secret Service coffee mug he gave me and it's never been used!

The Angelone family established the Albert Angelone Memorial Award to be given every year to the first junior Derby angler to weigh in a bonito.

"THERE ARE NO SECRETS ON THE WATER."

In the mid to late 90's after striped bass were declared fully recovered and before I moved to the Vineyard in 2002, I worked part time for a few years at Rivers End Bait and Tackle in Old Saybrook CT, even though it was forty five minute drive from my apartment outside of Hartford. It was owned by Pat Abate and Sherwood Lincoln, guys who had reputations of being two of the best all around fishermen in the northeast. I wanted to learn how to become a better striped bass fisherman and thought it might be a good way to pick up some tips.

Pat Abate doesn't fish like he once did, but in the seventies he was regarded as one of the top surf casters on the striper coast and I was in awe of the Shaefer Cup fishing trophies he displayed on the shelf behind the counter.

Pat never fished the Derby but is no stranger to the Vineyard. He once told me a story about a Halloween visit to the Island in the seventies with his friends Fred Hart and former Islander, Ken Vanderlaske. They fished the mussel bar at Squibnocket and enjoyed a special night with fish in the thirty to fifty pound range. The action was so good and the fish so big that Ken felt compelled to go home and return with his wife, Lori, who landed her personal best of 38 lbs. Pat's biggest that night was 51 lbs.

In 1995 Lori was a Derby Grand Leader for catching an 18.69 lb. blue-fish......on a fly rod.

Shortly after the furor over plover protection and subsequent beach closures began in the early nineties, Pat visited the Island with a group of friends and stayed at Judy Murphy's little compound at the opening to Shear Pen Pond on Chappy. In advance of their visit, they glued a few extra feathers on a Christmas tree ornament shaped like a bird, and Pat's friend and artist Mark Lewchik painted it to look like a piping plover. One afternoon, while their friend Mike Libman was at the surf fishing, they loosely buried it behind the front passenger tire of his vehicle, leaving just enough showing to remove any doubt about it being a plover.

Bart Cook was the Trustees Ranger and also a part time Edgartown policeman who liked to play tough cop. He approached the group and asked who the truck belonged to, pointing out it was parked in a restricted area. Pat said no problem they'd move it, then let him in on the joke and asked if he would play along.

Bart was all over the idea and informed Mike he was parked out of bounds and had killed an endangered bird in the process. Poor Mike was mortified just by the fact that he had killed the plover but became visibly more upset when Bart let him know in no uncertain terms that he was in big trouble and the possible penalties for the 'taking' of a piping plover was a fine of up to $25,000 and six months in jail. Pat said the usual outgoing and good natured Mike turned white as a ghost and was speechless until the rest of the group couldn't control their laughter any longer and relieved him of his anguish.

The other half of the ownership team at Rivers End was Sherwood Lincoln. Arguably, Sherwood was one of the best striped bass fishermen there ever was. He has more than fifty "50's" to his credit and recently wrote a great book titled "Striperman, Confessions of a Striped Bass Fisherman."

It was my job to open the shop at 5:00 AM on weekends and I was basically a fifty five year old stock boy. Rivers End was a short ride from the boat launch under the Baldwin Bridge on the Connecticut River and there was usually a line of fishermen waiting for me when I arrived shortly before five. Once I took care of the waiting customers my next job was to transfer hundreds of sandworms from flats of a gross into smaller boxes of a dozen. When I got ahead on that chore, it was packing bunker into bags of three, or plastic wrapping mackerel for individual sale. When things slowed a little, I would stock shelves or pack terminal tackle.

At my age, it was a tough way to get an education, but I was learning and although both guys were pretty closed mouth, I would listen very carefully to quiet conversations between Pat and Sherwood and their friends, as well as absorb their advice to customers. One of the most important things I learned was how much I didn't know.

When things were slow, which was rare, I would read the many books they had for sale or pop an instructional tape into the VCR. Although I rarely picked up a fly rod, one of the best and most well researched fishing books I ever read was "Flyrodding the Coast" by Ed Mitchell. Another good one was "Secrets of Surf Fishing at Night" by William A. Muller.

Many mornings I would get to the area around two in the morning, fish a local spot, and then show up in time to open the shop at five. There were a few instances when the fishing was so good it was very tough to leave, but Pat and Sherwood were sticklers for not making customers wait so I made sure I was there on time.

It took a long time for Pat to loosen up enough to start sharing fishing information with me and even then it was sparsely doled out. One of his favorite sayings was "there are no secrets on the water." He was and likely still is, the most closed mouthed fisherman I know, but in his opinion, it's very hard to keep a fishing spot a secret.

In today's world I think that's true, even during the Derby. Gone are the Derby days of old when anglers went to great lengths to keep their spots a secret. Back then guys would bury their catch, go back to cover drag marks in the sand and even drive around in circles until they lost anglers they thought were trying to tail them.

The legendary Sergei De Somov won four Derbys in the sixties including three with striped bass over fifty pounds. De Somov appeared to be a master of secrecy. In an article he once wrote for Salt Water Sportsman magazine, Derby Hall of Fame member Kib Bramhall described De Somov as the "Phantom of the Surf" because of his mysterious and secretive ways. He said, "nobody saw the man fish. If he saw headlights coming, even in the middle of a blitz, he would pack up and leave."

These days if someone has a good night it's more than likely that within a day or two the secret will be out and the place will get crowded. Fishermen love to talk and I recently heard someone say that three people can keep a secret but only if two of them are dead. That could apply to surf fishing on Martha's Vineyard.

Social media plays a big part in it. With cell phones and cameras it's very hard to keep a fishing spot a secret and it appears as though many of today's anglers are more interested in showing off their catch, or building a reputation of being the guy in the know than guarding their spot. Personally I find that egotistical and boring and can't quite understand it other than to say that egos play a big part in this sport. Humility seems to be lacking. The better fishermen are quiet about their catches and the places they fish. They are also humble about their success and let their record speak for them.

The Derby is a competition and why anyone would want to share a hot fishing spot with someone other than a most trusted friend is hard to comprehend. If a guy tells one person, and that person tells another, and then that person tells a friend, the word quickly spreads outward like a spider web. Does anyone think Bill Belichik would share his play book with Rex Ryan? I've been on the beach in the very early hours of the morning and seen camera flashes. Sure enough, the next day, photos appear on someone's Facebook page and the spot is burned. I'll freely share information the rest of the season but the Derby is another story!

Of course there are some spots that are difficult to keep secret. Tom Kieras and Ralph Peckham are bottom fishermen and regularly score in the Derby. In 2003, Tom won the Shore Bluefish Division and the Grand Prize Clay Family truck. He was also second in 2005. Ralph won the Shore Bluefish Division in 2008, was third in 1999 and 2009, and in 2013 was a Grand Prize key holder.

It's no secret where they fish and at least 100 vehicles pass them every day on their way to Leland's Point to make their 1,000 daily casts hoping to hit the false albacore lottery. Tom spends a lot of time surf fishing for sharks in FL and is the ultimate bait dunker. When he fishes the Derby he rarely fails to score. He watches the weather for what he feels are optimum conditions. He also keeps his eye on the Derby results and times his visits very carefully. When he's on the Island he and Ralph camp out almost every day at their spot on East Beach. They rarely deviate and have been very successful.

Martha's Vineyard has miles of fishable shoreline but access to much of it is difficult because it's privately owned either by an individual or an owners association. Many of the better places to fish require a long walk in or permission from the property owner to fish it. But after you've been around awhile you get a pretty good feel for where most of the hard core regulars fish and with real-time information available on the Derby's web-site, if someone starts scoring pins, it's usually not very difficult to figure out where those fish are being caught.

As far as I know, there is no secret shore spot for false albacore or bonito. Most of the anglers who target these speedsters spend their time on Chappy, the Lobsterville, Menemsha and Tashmoo jetties or the Memorial Wharf and Derby winning fish have come from all of these places. It's more important to observe the habits of these fish and try to be in the right place at the right time.

I learned my Derby secrecy lesson the hard way a number of years ago when I shared some information with a friend. Until the tide cycle changed, every night for almost a week stripers to the mid twenties would readily eat 2 oz. Super Strike "Mr. Hanky" clear amber darters and we were cleaning up on daily pins. I had to leave the Island for a couple of days, which is something I hate to do during the Derby, and while I was away he caught a thirty-three pound striper that temporarily put him into the overall division lead. It upset me to think I might have caught that fish. To rub salt into the wound, the morning after I returned, I arrived at first light just in time to see him and his friends walking off the beach carrying weighable stripers, some with more than one. Ordinarily that wouldn't have bothered me so much but it was the Derby and they were also seen by a number of other people so the secret was out.

Since then I try to keep my mouth shut about any success I might have with stripers, particularly during the Derby.

Even good striped bass anglers fail to guard their spots. A few years back, a guy had some great early success throwing a Steve McKenna rigged Sluggo at the mussel bar at Squibnocket. He ended up winning the Shore Striped Bass Division but within a couple of days after he caught his winning fish, the word got out and many of the local sharpies showed up on the bar, all throwing McKenna rigged Sluggo's.

Phil Hennig from Simsbury, CT is a younger friend of mine who for almost twenty years has joined me to fish the Derby. With family responsibilities and the limitations of living more than an hour from the very restrictive and private CT coast, it's about the only time he fishes all year.

In 2002, Phil and I were doing well drifting eels on an early morning falling tide at the Wasque Rip. The ORV trail was closed due to erosion and the only way to access the Rip was from the Fishermen's parking lot and for three nights we had the place to ourselves. We would station ourselves right at the beginning of the rip line, cast the eel up current and let it swim toward the bottom, and then drift it out in the Rip for a thirty count before we would start a slow retrieve as we walked west to catch up with it.

We were hammering the fish and scoring daily pins and not a soul knew we were there until one night we saw a light coming down the stairway from the parking lot. We already had two fish in the low twenties on the beach but were looking for the Derby winner. When we saw the light there was a brief discussion of what to do. Do we keep fishing and run the risk of being outed, do we hide the fish and keep fishing, or do we just leave? We agreed that the fishing was just too good to leave and had to stay. So Phil grabbed the fish, made an end run around the back of the approaching angler and hustled the fish to the parking lot and security of the cooler.

While he was gone the unknown angler set up and started casting about fifty yards to my right and until Phil returned I continued to have success, as almost every drift produced a fish. Only now I had to be stealthy about it. Instead of unhooking a fish on the sand, I turned my back to the angler and tried to make it look like I was changing lures by holding the fish straight up and down at chest level while removing the circle hook. Even after Phil's return we continued to catch fish until the first rays of false dawn started to lighten the sky. During this time we never saw the interloper put a fish on the beach.

When it came time to leave we were gathering our gear when the guy walked over and asked if we had any luck. Of course we told him no. He then asked me if I lived on Windsor Drive. When I told him I did, he introduced himself as Jim Cornwell and said he lived in the new house just down the street from me. I still didn't have the heart or the desire to let him in our secret. He had been throwing a Gibbs Bottle Darter and said he never even had a hit. The next night and for a couple of nights after we went back and again had the place to ourselves. And we hammered fish!

Over the next few years I got to know Jim very well and he became a close friend and someone I greatly respect as an angler as well as a person. It took a long time for me to tell him what really happened at the Rip that night. I was driving by his house one day when I saw him doing some work near the end of his driveway. I stopped and we naturally started talking fishing and I finally revealed the story. His lower jaw dropped and his mouth hung open. He was speechless and just stared at me in disbelief. When he finally started to talk, he just kind of shook his head, and I hate to say it; it was almost comical. He called his wife, Joyce, out of the house and told her the story but by now he was finding the ironic humor in it and was laughing. Joyce even ran into the house to get her camera and took a picture. She called it "the confession."

In case you are feeling sorry for Jim-**don't**. He caught the largest shore bonito that year and although he didn't win the boat, he was a Grand Prize leader. He was a Grand Prize leader again in 2008 after catching the largest shore false albacore. Only a small percentage of Derby anglers have been fortunate enough to have even one chance at the Grand Prize and still fewer have done it twice.

───❦───

Since I moved to the Island I've done my due diligence and worked very hard to learn the ins and outs of my bass spots. I've fished a lot of places but unlike the old days when I would chase reports all over the Island, I have settled on four or five spots that I know intimately. At my age it's important to be efficient and, like an old striper, use whatever energy I have left, wisely. I try to plan my work and work my plan and scout all of my spots before the Derby so when the bell rings, I can be on the fish. I have fished them at all stages of the tide and in all conditions and have a pretty good feel for when stripers will be at these locations. I rarely deviate, especially during the Derby, as they all produce fish sometime during the event. If I don't find them in one place, I can usually find them at another.

Most of the places I fish are not secret at all but during the Derby I try to time the tides and fish them in the early morning hours and rarely run into another angler. Two spots are on private property and require a very long walk in.

In 2012 I found a new spot. Roger Ardanowski is a non-fishing friend of mine who vacations here with his family in late August. While he was here he sent me a picture of a freshly dead, half eaten 15" striper and asked what I thought could bite it in half so cleanly. It was obvious to me that it was the work of a big bluefish and during a low tide a few days later I walked the beach in the area he found the fish.

As a surf angler, what I found was pretty amazing. Along a stretch of what appeared to be a featureless beach, was a nice perpendicular bar with current flowing by setting up a deep bowl and back eddy behind it. In addition, it was the only place on a mile of sandy beach that showed any sign of structure in the form of small stones and shell debris. I decided to fish it one night before the Derby and

was not surprised when my darter was eaten by school stripers up to 30".

I tucked the information away and on day two of the Derby fished the rising tide there around three in the morning and was rewarded with a half dozen stripers up to fifteen pounds before the tide changed around first light. I never saw another soul in an area that should have been loaded with surf anglers and I attributed it to being the second day of the Derby and the possibility that many had burned themselves out or not had any luck the night before.

As light crept into the sky, I moved about a quarter mile away to a nice bowl which had some slack water just inside the east flowing current. I threw out a chunk of bunker and it wasn't in the water more than ten minutes when the rod doubled over and line peeled off the Shimano Baitrunner. The fish was an 11.5 lb. bluefish which I quickly threw in the cooler and got out of there. The fish took the overall lead ahead of the smallish 6 lb. leader that had been weighed in on the opening day. It was a daily first place winner and held up for the weekly prize as well and surprisingly held down the top spot on the shore bluefish leader board for more than two weeks.

I continued to stealthily fish the spot for the entire Derby, usually in the early hours of the morning but also a few times at dusk which was risky because of the angling traffic in the area. As the Derby wore on some bigger fish moved in and in week two of the event I scored my striped bass Hat Trick over four consecutive days. I also won the Top Rod award that year with seven daily pins. Five came from that spot.

I did break my own rule and took Bob Clay there one night. Bob brought his fly rod and caught a 13.25 lb. striper that he rushed off to weigh-in. It put him into the Shore Fly-Rod Division lead for about an hour until our good friend Joe Dart came in with a 13.61 lb. fish. The next night Bob went back and caught a 15.05 lb. striper that put him back into the lead and held on to win the division.

Bob used to laugh at me when I gave him information and ask that he not share it but as far as I know he hasn't told a soul about where he caught his prize winning fish.

TEAM McRAT

I was a member of the Derby Committee in 2008 when the decision was made to add team competition to the event. A subcommittee met to set parameters and decided upon a two person team format in both the shore and boat division, consistent with other events in the grand scheme of the Derby. Anglers would be allowed to pick their own team-mates as well as name their respective team, and did not have to fish together. For the first few years, there would only be a first place award handed out in the form of a simple plaque and the winning team would be determined by the overall total weight of the four eligible species, with the heaviest of each specie per team counting toward the aggregate total.

I thought it was a great idea and immediately started thinking about who I could partner with. I felt that if I could find a teammate who possessed the same Derby mind set and would be willing to compare notes and share information, we might be able to win the event. My friends Pat Toomey and Keith McArt immediately came to mind. Although both were more than twenty years younger than me, they were outstanding surf anglers, good guys and good fishing partners.

Pat and his wife Polly are the proprietors of the very popular Among the Flowers restaurant in Edgartown. I met him late one night at the Edgartown Pond opening in 2002, the year I moved here.

The pond had been cut open a couple of days before and the fishing was good. I was having a fair night but saw this guy wailing on fish just a few yards away from me. He seemed to be hooking up three or four times for every fish I put on the beach. When we finally met on the sand while unhooking a fish, I noticed he was throwing a 2 oz. Danny just like I was but using a conventional rod and reel. I could only surmise that he was getting it out just a little farther and that it was making the difference.

He introduced himself and we seemed to hit it off immediately. He told me he was born on the Island and had been fishing the surf since he was a small boy. He said that when he was a kid he used to hitchhike to the beach to fish and would often be picked up by Ed Amaral, who was a mutual friend to both of us. After an hour or so of him putting on a clinic as he likes to say, he said he had to leave as he had to open the restaurant in just a few hours. He told me to stop in the shop and have a coffee with him sometime. He left around 1:00 AM and shortly after the bite really picked up. Until it got light I bailed on fish to the high teens and went through two packages of 9" Sluggos before the action finally died. It was one of the best nights I ever had.

I went back the next couple of nights and Pat was there each time. As the week wore on the fishing slowed, but we caught fish every night and got to know each other a little better. I didn't get a good look at his face until I stopped in the restaurant a week later.

Pat is a tireless and fanatical surf fisherman and about as intense and competitive as they come, but unfortunately for him, can only burn the midnight fishing candle until late June every year when he starts serving dinner at Among the Flowers. In 2005 when On the Water magazine loosely resurrected the former Shaefer Beer Striper Cup fishing tournament, Pat won the Surf Angler of the Year award by catching the five heaviest striped bass - and he did it in five consecutive weeks!

During the 2013 Derby, Pat found some big fish and his daughter Emma won both the shore junior striped bass and bluefish division and his six year old son Chase swept the same mini-junior divisions. In addition, Emma won the Top Rod Award for juniors with a total of six pins. At the Derby Awards Ceremony the Toomey family, Pat, Polly, Emma, and Chase was awarded the Beaulieu/Loud Memorial Award for the family that best exemplifies togetherness and sportsmanship.

———⚬❀⚬———

Keith McArt is also an intense and tireless angler. Keith's family has a summer home in Oak Bluffs and before he got married and started raising a family of his own, Keith would take whatever vacation time he had and telecommute from Oak Bluffs so he could fish almost the entire Derby.

He would fish an insane number of hours and make thousands of casts looking for that one big albie or elusive bonito. Night would often find him fishing entire tides at Wasque then travelling up island to fish tides there. When exhaustion finally took its toll he would grab a few hours of sleep in the front seat of his small black jeep and when he couldn't take it anymore, would enjoy the luxury of a few hours on a real mattress in his Oak Bluffs home. On more than one occasion, during the twenty five mile trip up island, he would pull off the road to grab a power nap, many nights up to four times.

In addition to being about as intense as they come, Keith is also one of the best surf casters I know, and a great Derby fisherman. I met him on Chappy in 2003 the year he won the All Tackle Shore Grand Slam and placed third in the All-Tackle Shore Bonito Division. In 2004 he was a Grand Leader and key holder for catching the largest All Tackle Shore Striped Bass with a 42.46 lb. fish, and in 2005 caught a 42.54 lb. striped bass, which was second to Leo Lecuyer's 45.18 lb. Grand Leader. As far as I can determine, Keith and Leo are the only shore anglers who have recorded back to back forty pound stripers since they were re-introduced into the Derby in 1993.

At the risk of losing a good friend, I asked Keith to be my partner and was glad he agreed as it turned out to be a good decision.

Twenty four teams entered the shore team competition the first year, and thanks primarily to Keith's efforts, Team McRat won the inaugural event by more than fifteen pounds over our closest competitor. Keith carried us with a 36.46 lb. striper, a 9.52 lb. false albacore and a 7.05 lb. bonito that picked up his Deadly Dick as he started to retrieve again after untangling a braid attack. My only contribution to the 62.76 lb. aggregate total was a 9.72 lb. bluefish.

His striper and bonito both placed second in their respective All Tackle Shore Divisions and he won the All Tackle Shore Grand Slam as well as the Abe Williams Memorial Award for being the first angler of the year to record a shore slam.

2008 was also the year I turned 65 and moved into the Senior Division. Coincidently, my street number is 65, as is my Derby badge number. My wedding anniversary is June fifth or 6/5. I'm not very superstitious, and I'm not sure if some of Keith's luck rubbed off on me, but the numbers sure fell into place. Not only did I make my first trip onto the awards stage after a long absence, I walked up a number of other times, and although I didn't contribute much to our team, I won awards for the largest shore striped bass and bluefish caught by a senior and seven daily pins which brought me the Shore Top Rod Award.

Between us that year, Keith and I made eleven trips to the stage. As we were walking off the stage after receiving the team award, I heard someone remark "those two guys shouldn't be teammates." It was one of the best compliments I ever received!

Keith and I won the team competition again in 2009 but it was not the cake walk of the previous year. On the second night of the Derby I weighed in a striper that was just short of 25 lbs. and a few days later a 6.52 lb. bluefish that gave us the early team lead, but I was having problems catching a weighable albie.

Keith and Andrea were expecting their first child and the due date was October 1st so he was limited to just one week of fishing, with the distinct possibility of having even that time cut short. But as was always the case he was making the most of his time and hitting it even harder than usual. In the limited time he was here, he caught more than 100 stripers but not many pushed the scale much over the fifteen pound mark. In addition, the albie fishing was slow as was the chunking on East Beach and lousy weather wasn't helping matters much.

Two weeks into the Derby we found ourselves sitting in second place behind Team Rusty Hooks who had put up a 24.23lb. striper and an 8.59 lb. bluefish and really stuck the knife in with a 5.97 lb. bonito for an aggregate weight of 38.79 lbs. Team McRat was in second place but far behind with an aggregate total of 31.57 lbs..

Bob (Hawkeye) Jacobs and Ron McKee comprise Rusty Hooks and are as hard core as they come. They are also charter 'Wharf Rat' members, meaning most of their daylight fishing hours are spent chasing bonito and false albacore at the Memorial Wharf in Edgartown. In addition, both are former winners or have placed in the top three of the All Tackle Shore Grand Slam competition.

Hawkeye won the division in 2001 and 2002 and was third in 1995 and 1998. In addition, he caught the third Largest Shore False Albacore in 1997 and was third again in 2001. He also became an instant legend one year when he was fighting an albie off Memorial Wharf that got hung up on the Pied Piper passenger ferry which was tied up there. With rod in hand he hopped on board and made several unsuccessful attempts to free the fish, then persuaded fellow

Wharf Rat Dennis Gough to fetch a mask and snorkel from his car. He stripped down to his skivvies, donned the gear and left the rod leaning against the rail with the bail open under Dennis's watchful eye, and jumped overboard. When he got under the boat, he still could not do anything to free the fish, and finally gave up.

When asked how the crew reacted to all of this, Bob said the Captain was "actually real nice about it and I think amused by the whole thing," but a crewman who he believes was the Purser "went berserk on me. I can't tell you what she said because I totally tuned her out. It was a nice fish!"

A week later she wrote a letter to the Martha's Vineyard Times claiming he was a nut, and "not of sound mind!"

Very early one morning in June of 2012, Bob was fishing off the Big Bridge on the Oak Bluffs/Edgartown Road when he heard a loud scraping noise and saw a car go off the road and into the water. Not being the owner of a cell phone, he tried unsuccessfully to flag down a passing car but failing that, ran down to the riprap along the edge just in time to reach out a hand as the driver stumbled toward shore. The car, which was balanced on a rock, went over the edge and submerged completely.

In recognition and appreciation of his efforts, the Derby Committee bought him a cell phone!

Hawkeyes's partner is Ron McKee and I think it's safe to say he lives to fish. Ron resides in Buxton, ME and when he's not fishing works as a prison guard. He calls himself the "Striper Maine-iac" and served his apprenticeship under the guidance of the late Bob Pond, the founder of Atom Lures. He now produces his own line of lures appropriately called "Striper Maine-iac Lures."

In the fall, Ron tries to fish the entire five weeks of the Derby and rooms with Hawkeye. He hunts all day for albies and bonito, grabs a few hours of sleep and then walks miles of beach casting for striped bass. When the Derby ends, he sometimes hits the road and follows the striper migration as it moves through Rhode Island, New York and New Jersey. Ron is a grand slammer to the nth degree. He won the event in 1999, was third in 2002, second in 2007 and third again in 2009. He also caught the second largest shore bonito in 1997 and the third largest in 1999.

To say they are a formidable team would almost be an understatement and before the 2009 Derby began, they publicly expressed their intention to win the team competition.

On Saturday September 29, Keith was down to his last day of fishing. He fished a tide on Chappy then headed to Lobsterville where he grabbed two hours of sleep before he started his albie quest at 5:45 AM. It was a miserable morning with a northeast wind blowing almost in his face at about twenty knots. There were whitecaps on the water and nobody was hooking up and slowly the crowd thinned out as anglers gave up, but Keith, John Schillinger, Wilson Kerr, and a couple of others kept at it.

Around 9:30 that morning, I was sitting at the computer doing the daily deposit at Larry's when I got a call from Keith who very excitedly told me that he had just caught a big albie. We talked about the possibility of making it down in time for the morning weigh-in but decided it was unlikely that he could get there by ten so we agreed the best strategy was to get the fish on ice as soon as possible as albies are known to dry out and lose weight. When I asked him how big it was, all he said was "big" and that it would get us back into the team lead. We agreed to meet at Derby headquarters at 8:00 PM and he asked me to please bring a camera. During the day, the buzz among the Island fishing community heated up and the weight estimates ranged from thirteen to fifteen pounds. I couldn't wait to see the fish.

Barbara and I arrived at the weigh-in before 8:00 PM and waited for Keith to show up. We were inside when he arrived and just by the rise in the noise level outside, we knew he was there. When he walked in the door I was shocked at the size of the fish. The albie was huge and larger than most people there had ever seen. He put it on the scale and it weighed 16.55 lbs., ranking it as the second largest shore division false albacore ever recorded and right behind the 16.71 lb. fish caught by Dennis Gough off Memorial Wharf in 2005.

The fish was a long and lean 'runner.' Don MacGillivary's mount of his Derby and state record albie sits high on the wall at Larry's Tackle Shop. Many who saw Keith's albie that night believe that if it had more girth, it would easily have eclipsed the big 19.39 lb. fish.

The weight of Keith's single fish was the equivalent of catching a fair size albie and a good size bonito, and in addition to almost guaranteeing him a key and still another shot at the Grand Prize, put Team McRat back in team division lead with a total of 48.28 lbs..

During the last two weeks of the Derby both the fishing and the weather tanked and the event ended with a two day nor'easter. I worked hard, played the winds and fished the tides at all of my favorite spots with hardly any luck at all. I finally came to realize that since we already had a pretty good striper on the

board, as well as Keith's leading albie, the best chance to add some weight to our lead was to catch a bluefish larger than the 6.52 lb. fish we had already weighed in. I spent much of the last two weeks of the Derby dunking bait on East Beach, but for the entire stretch I was only able to add a measly .10 lbs. to our weight with a 6.62 lb. bluefish.

It was slow and agonizingly boring. I hated it and thought more than once about throwing in the towel and quitting. But fish were occasionally being caught on both sides of me and not more than fifty yards away the entire time so I hung in there. Meanwhile, McKee and Hawkeye kept adding to their weight. McKee caught a bigger bass and Hawkeye was finding some bluefish, and they had narrowed our lead to less than .30 of a pound.

Around 5:00 PM on the last night of the Derby, I was dunking bait on East Beach along with a number of other guys when Hawkeye pulled into a narrow space just a few yards away from me and started doing the same thing. Although we know each other well, I was totally freaked out by his presence and the possibility that he could catch the winning fish right in front of me. I could only nod a greeting and we never said a word to each other the entire time he was there.

It was head to head fishing competition. It was getting dark and I hadn't had a hit in two hours and no one else had either. I was tired and miserable and wanted the Derby to be over. I also wanted to go home but wasn't about to leave and run the risk of Hawkeye catching what could be my fish. I called my wife and told her I was not leaving until one of us caught a fish or he left. Finally at around 8:00 PM it was down to Hawkeye and me and after what seemed an eternity Hawkeye packed it in and left. I breathed a sigh of relief, reeled in my lines and called Barbara to tell her I would be home soon. It was over-we had won!!!

I found out later that Hawkeye just moved to another spot and fished right up to the last possible moment. Knowing Hawkeye and how competitive he is and how hard he fishes, I was not surprised.

We ended up winning the team competition but only by a scant .20 of a pound or slightly more than three ounces out of a total weight of almost fifty pounds. I was not as elated as I was the previous year and although happy that we had won, the win did not bring me a lot of satisfaction. I did not have a good Derby and was unhappy with myself for even thinking about quitting.

Two days after he got home on September 30, Keith and Andrea brought Sabrina McArt into this world. When they came back for the awards ceremony, he brought her to the Derby weigh-in and took a picture of her on the official scale. She weighed less than his albie but is a keeper nonetheless. A couple of years ago, the McArts presented Sabrina with her sister Adele, only this time the timing was a little better.

THE DARK SIDE

IF YOU ARE in any kind of a relationship for thirty years you are going to have your ups and downs as well as see the good and bad in it, and the Derby is no exception. I had a plumber do some work on our house before the 2013 Derby and learned he was a fly fisherman and a pretty good one at that. I spoke with him a few days before the Derby and asked him if he was all set. He told me no, he probably would not even enter. I was surprised and when I asked why, he said he felt the event brought out the worst in people. When I thought about what he said, I realized there was some truth to it. Like many good things in life, there is sometimes a dark side to it as well and during my thirty years of Derby participation, there has been some bad to go along with much good. When you put a valuable prize on the line as well as a lifetime of bragging rights, it's bound to happen. I've witnessed and experienced some of it.

Barbara and I always try to go to the weigh-in on the last night of the Derby to be there with the nervous Derby leaders, listen to stories or see if there are any last minute histrionics. One year, we were standing inside when I guy I knew only by face recognition from my days at Rivers End in CT walked in the main doors. I had never seen him on the island before but he recognized me and walked toward me with his eyes glued on the Grand Leader board in back of the scale. He asked how big the leading bluefish was and I redirected him back to the board which he studied for a minute or so, then walked back out the doors.

There was suddenly some excitement outside and he walked back in with two very big bluefish that he flopped on the counter. I don't remember the exact weights but they each were over sixteen pounds and big enough to take over as the Grand Leader in the boat division.

After he left and the excitement settled a bit committee member Porky Francis, who had seen me talking to him, walked over and asked if I knew the guy. I told him my story and he said that most local captains had been out all day and none of them had found fish anywhere close to the size of the two he brought in. He also said that he had arrived in a taxi and if the Derby committee found out he had been picked up at the ferry dock, he was going to be in big trouble.

When we got to the ceremony on Sunday the guy was nowhere to be found and I was told that when confronted by the committee and informed that if he won the truck but it was determined that his fish were caught out of bounds, he could be charged with a felony. He voluntarily withdrew the fish. Later that afternoon I learned from a friend that a blitz of big bluefish had been taking place along the southern Rhode Island beaches the day he showed up. I haven't seen him here since!

———⚬⚬⚬———

1990 was a year after the moratorium on striped bass was lifted but tight restrictions were still in place and it would be a few years before they were reintroduced into the Derby as an eligible species. The minimum legal size limit for striped bass that year was 34" and the daily bag limit one.

Late one stormy afternoon that year I was approaching the Cape Poge jetties from the north and found breaking fish that appeared to be albies. I pulled up between the jetties just in time to see a very excited angler beach a striped bass that appeared to be well under the 34" minimum. I said something like the usual "nice fish" and started to get out of my vehicle when the guy walked away with it. I confronted him with the fact that I didn't think the fish was 34" and he said he didn't care, he was taking it anyway. A few years later the Derby committee imposed a two year ban on the guy for high-grading.

The story doesn't quite end there because after that little exchange the fish were still breaking. I made my way out to the end of the jetty and on the second cast with a 1 oz. Hammer hooked an albie. The fish took off on a screaming run toward the Cape Poge lighthouse and just melted the 10# Ande mono off my Symetre 4000 reel. I was momentarily paralyzed by the sheer speed of the run but came to my senses and it took me less than a minute to make my way off the jetty in an attempt to run it down. But the fish never stopped or even slowed and by the time I got back on the sand, the entire spool of line had disappeared.

Don MacGillivary set the state and Derby false albacore record that year with a 19.39 lb. fish that he hooked off Cape Poge!

On another occasion before the striper bag limit went to two fish, there were some very big bass being weighed in on a daily basis and rumored to be coming from the Tisbury Pond opening. I checked the tide and decided to fish it. Around eleven one night I made the drive down the long dirt road to the Trustees parking lot and was surprised to see only a few cars there when I arrived. I unloaded my gear and made my way out along the edge of the pond and when I walked over the dune onto the front beach, the scene I took in could easily have been the subject of a Ray Ellis painting.

The moon was full in the southern sky and lit up the beach like a spotlight. There were at least half-dozen vehicles on the beach and a long line of rods tipped with glow sticks stuck in sand spikes. With the exception of a few guys back lit by the moon and fishing the outer sand bar fifty yards in front of the opening, no one seemed to be plugging or throwing eels. Out in front of the guys on the bar was a boat that was close enough so that when it swung on its anchor line I was able to see the glow of its instruments.

I took in the scene for a few minutes then hooked an eel and tossed it into the outflow and left the bail open. It hadn't drifted for more than a ten count when I felt a bump that signaled a pick-up. I let it go for a few more seconds, closed the bail and set the hook. It was a decent fish which felt even better because I was hauling it in against the out-flowing current. After a nice fight, I beached it and dragged it out of the wash and put a tape measure to it. It was 43" and I figured close to thirty pounds. As I was unhooking it Steve Amaral walked over and agreed it was in the thirty pound range. I gathered up my stuff, hooked the fish on my drag rope and was back at my car less than an hour after I arrived. The fish weighed 29.5 lbs. and wasn't big enough to get me into the overall top three or take over the weekly lead but it was a daily pin winner.

I went back the next night and the scene was almost exactly the same, only this time I didn't have the first cast magic and the spot I was in the night before was occupied by someone tossing eels. I moved down the beach and couldn't get the drift I wanted but continued to fish anyway hoping I could eventually move back to where I was the night before.

A short time after I arrived I noticed one of the fly fishermen on the outer bar was hooked up and after a long battle, beat the fish and was holding it up against his leg appearing to be discussing it with the guy next to him. A few more minutes passed before he turned and walked back against the outflow toward the beach and passed me on his way in. As he went by, I congratulated him and started fishing again. The fish looked to be in the mid to high teen range.

A period of time passed and he came walking by me in the opposite direction toward the outer bar. "You going to try it again?" I asked. I didn't hear his reply against the noise from the surf but out he went.

He was soon hooked up again only this time he was retreating back toward me while fighting the fish. It took him at least fifteen minutes to work it against the outflow and close to the beach. As he got even with me I remarked about catching another one and he said, "yes, only now I have a problem because this one is bigger than the first." I remember saying something like "yes you do" and I started fishing again.

I continued to throw my eel but was curious as to what he was going to do, so I kept looking back. He dragged the fish up the beach and unhooked it then returned to the outflow not more than twenty feet behind me and started to revive a fish that I assumed was the first one. He worked hard at it for a very long time then finally walked back to the beach without it, picked up the remaining fish and was out of there. The fish he was trying to revive simply disappeared in the outflow.

The next morning I checked the leader board at Derby headquarters and saw that the fish he weighed tipped the scales at twenty five pounds and took the lead in the shore flyrod striped bass division, knocking my friend Chip Bergeron into second. I thought about filing an official grievance but since I had no proof that the fish didn't miraculously swim away, I didn't, but based on the amount of time it took to fight the second fish and then get the first one back to the water, I doubt it survived.

Finally, a few years back I arrived at Derby headquarters around 9:00 AM one morning to weigh a mid-teen size striper I had caught the night before. A number of us, including Bob Clay, had been fishing the same area and Bob had weighed a 24 lb. fish just a few minutes earlier which gave him a temporary lead in the Senior Division until Tony Rezendez knocked him off just a half hour later.

I put my fish on the scale and when Roy Langley read the weight to Robyn Jobert at the computer, a loud celebration erupted from behind me. I looked around to see this guy pumping his fist, loudly yelling "*yes, yes, yes*". I couldn't believe it. A guy I thought was my friend took great delight in the fact that his fish was .17 of a pound (3 ounces) heavier than mine. If the fish was still in his hands, I think he would have spiked it. Even the volunteers behind the counter were staring in stunned silence.

The late Paul Brown, founder and former coach of the Cleveland Browns, once said, "When you win say nothing. When you lose say less." I've been competing in sports and sporting events for most of my life but this was the worst case of poor sportsmanship I ever encountered!

"THE THRILL OF VICTORY...AND THE AGONY OF DEFEAT"

BEFORE THERE WERE twelve ESPN channels and every major network had its own sports channel, ABC's popular Wide World of Sports would lead off their weekly show with an opening scene showing an Olympic athlete admiring his gold medal and then a ski jumper falling horrendously off the end of a jump. The voice-over in the background featured the late sportscaster Jim McKay uttering the famous phrase *"the thrill of victory...and the agony of defeat'*. The show lasted thirty seven years.

In the thirty years I've been fishing the Derby I've been fortunate enough not to have suffered any major mishaps that caused physical injury but I've suffered my share of ups and downs and the thrill of victory and the agony of defeat. The Derby will do that to you.

For a good many years I would enter the Derby with high expectations of success which most times turned into total disappointment when after ten days of fishing, I would leave the Island with my tail tucked between my legs. I always put a lot of pressure on myself because I set the bar way too high and I would feel the pain for weeks after and be absolutely miserable. Even after moving here permanently it wasn't until I started to figure things out and experienced some minor success that I started to feel better about myself. And now at my age I've finally gotten to the point where Derby success is important but doesn't really matter all that much anymore. I hope my competitive drive never dies but these days the important thing to me is that I'm still walking on this earth and able to fish this wonderful event.

My only real claim to fame and *thrill of victory* in the Derby came more than twenty years ago in 1992, and was about the closest I ever came to being a Grand Leader. I had spent ten days here fishing without much success and again went home disappointed. A week or two later my son came up with a bunch of friends to fish and party their way through a week and they invited me back for a long weekend.

Saturday morning was a sunny, flat calm day and there were a number of guys fishing the area around the Cape Poge jetties. On our trip out along the beach we stopped to talk with a few people and no one had caught a thing and there were no signs of fish anywhere. We had been fishing for at least an hour just to the north of the jetties when I made a cast and let my 1 oz. Hammer drop to a ten count. When I started to retrieve it I got a hit and had a fish take off on a screaming run toward the lighthouse. I literally ran the fish down and after a long fight with a drag that was set way too loose, slid a big bonito onto the sand. I had caught bonito before but this one had a whole different look to it. We wrapped it in a wet towel, threw it in the cooler along with whatever cold beer and ice we had and raced off to the weigh- in. The fish weighed 9.11 lbs. and went straight to the top of the All Tackle leader board and remained there until the Derby's end, but I lost the Grand Leader glory to a fly fisherman who caught a 9.92 lb. fish.

But bonito have also been the cause of much anguish for me. As I mentioned in a previous chapter, I consider the winners of the Grand Slam to be the best fishermen on the Island during the Derby. Anyone who can win the Grand Slam Division must devote an extraordinary amount of time to accomplish it and possess a great deal of angling knowledge and skills.

For years, it was always my goal to win the Shore Grand Slam. I even had dreams of doing it all in one day, something that's never been done by a shore angler and accomplished by boat anglers only three times in Derby history, twice by Pat Jenkinson and once by John Schillinger.

Catching the other three species was relatively easy and I did that on a number of occasions but could not catch the elusive 'bone.'

My inability to achieve it even after I started fishing the entire five weeks of the event led to much frustration and major disappointment. A couple of years my 'three fish' aggregate weight total even without the bonito was enough to win the event which made things even worse. East Beach, the Cape Pogue Jetties, Lobsterville, the Rip, it didn't matter, I couldn't catch a bonito.

One year, I had a bead on them below the bluffs on East Chop. Every morning for almost a week they would show up about a hundred yards off the beach, make a run toward the shore and then move toward Vineyard Haven Harbor. No one else knew they were there but I couldn't catch one.

Another year my friend Bob Clay caught one at the Cape Pogue jetties and I was fishing less than six feet away from him. He finished third in the All Tackle Shore Bonito Division.

In 2008 I finally achieved my 'Slam' and led the event for more than a week only to end up in fourth place and off the division leader board. I was happy to get my Grand Slam pin, but not finishing in the top three after leading the event was painful. I haven't caught a bonito since!

Striped bass have also provided their share of wins and losses for me over the years. 1992 was the year the Derby started to reintroduce striped bass into the Derby after a seven year absence and the year Bob Lane caught a 51 lb. fish at 'Carl's Rock'.

The day after I caught the big bonito that year I was driving down South Beach in the area of the Oyster Pond when I saw fish breaking within casting distance. I started throwing a popper and had 30" to 35" stripers all over it. I chased the fish on foot until they moved down the beach and out of range with the popper then ran back to my vehicle and caught up with them but changed out the popper for a 3 oz. Kastmaster. I put all I could into the next cast and had a huge fish explode on it almost as soon as it hit the water. I set the hook and knew immediately it was a big fish, bigger than anything I ever had on before. The fish took off on a very long run then settled down to the point where I was able to work it to within a few yards of me and swimming parallel to the beach. I kept it in front of me and worked it closer still, but suddenly felt it move to the bottom, offer some weird sideways resistance, shake its head, and it was gone. When I reeled in the Kastmaster it had a small strand of grass on it. I think the fish rubbed its nose in the sand and dislodged the single hook lure!

On the second night of the Derby a few years back I was in the rocks on the North Shore drifting eels on an outgoing tide when I hooked another very big fish. Aided by the current, the fish took off on a long run that I was able to slow and finally turn, but I was waist deep in a breaking surf and could not do much to move toward the fish so I had no choice but to heave and haul on it. Suddenly, the unthinkable happened - the circle hook pulled. I could not believe it. I stood there shaking for a while then slunk back to the beach and almost puked. If I hadn't made arrangements to meet Pat Toomey there, I would have gone straight home. When Pat arrived ten minutes later he found me sitting on a rock still shaking. I started to fish again and even managed a small fish but my heart just wasn't in it and I soon left.

Scott Tomkins won the Shore Striped Bass Division that year with a 40.12 lb. fish, but there is very little doubt in my mind that the fish I lost was in the forty pound range!

That same year, on the second to last day of the Derby, they popped the Tisbury Pond open. Many times when they open a pond, it takes a day or two for the word get out but the Derby is the exception. The parking lot was almost full when I arrived at the Long Point parking lot at one the next morning and there had to be fifteen to twenty vehicles there. I made the mile long 'hump' out to the beach but was relegated to a spot at the end of a line of anglers, a hundred yards to the east of the opening and outflow. Most guys were plugging but there were also a few fly fishing. I had hoped to drift eels into the outflow but that was out of the question so I started throwing an old metal lipped jointed needle fish that my neighbor Chuck Wendel had given me. The fishing was slow and I didn't see many lights going on but occasionally someone would slide a smallish fish onto the beach and I did manage to catch a couple of small schoolies myself.

The crowd slowly thinned out and finally by 3:00 AM I was the only one left on the beach. I moved to the opening which by now was flowing slowly out of the pond but still fast enough to drift an eel toward the outer bar. As the tide dropped a nice perpendicular bar had formed and I carefully made my way out as far as I dared. On my third drift with an eel I hooked and lost a decent fish but the next drift produced another one that appeared to be to be in the low twenties. I left it on the beach and waded out again but by then the tide had turned and water was flowing back into the pond.

I weighed the fish the next morning and when weigh master Roy Langley read the weight to Maria Plese who was the weigh station administrator at the time, she looked up from the computer and said; "oh a new Grand Leader!" **"What?"** "Yes a new *senior* leader!" The fish was only in the low twenties but I had conveniently forgotten that I became a senior citizen earlier that summer.

The striper not only hung on to win the senior division but also won a daily pin which gave me seven for the year, and enough to win the Shore Division Top Rod Award. I also won the Senior Shore Bluefish Division and Keith McArt and I won the Team Competition.

Even bluefish have provided measures of agony and ecstasy for me during the Derby. If you've gotten this far, you already read about my inability to catch a 22" bluefish to achieve a Grand Slam one year.

A number of years ago I was throwing eels on the soft side of the Cape Poge Gut, which is not highly regarded by Derby fishermen as a place that gives up big stripers. But if you're a pin junkie like I am, it can be a pretty consistent place to catch stripers up to twenty five pounds as well as an occasional big bluefish. In years past, but post Derby, my friends Paul Schultz and Bob McKay have each caught fifty pound bass there!

I was having success that night catching mid teen size stripers when I hooked something that felt much heavier. It made a couple of short runs down current and as I worked it toward me, it felt like a very big fish. I was able to get it fairly close when the line suddenly went slack and it was gone. When I reeled in the rest of the line and checked the leader, it was cut cleanly right above where the hook had been. It had been bitten off by a big bluefish. Since that night I rarely throw an eel without a four inch piece of 60# black wire above the hook. The bass could care less about the wire and I've never had another bluefish bite off a hook.

The 2012 Derby held yet another "*thrill of victory and agony of defeat*" for me. On the second night of the event, I caught an eleven pound bluefish that took the overall lead and held on for more than two weeks. I had no illusions of winning the whole thing with a fish that size but when you are in that position you always hope for a small miracle.

A week or so later, Phil Hennig and I took our friend Holly Mercier fishing for false albacore at Leland's Point and Holly caught her first ever shore albie. Phil was having some equipment problems so I loaned him my nine foot Marsh Bryan special. He soon hooked a fish and judging by the bend in the rod, it looked like a good one. He did a great job fighting it and the fish very grudgingly came toward the beach. When he got it close I asked him if it had made any runs and he said just short ones. I told him I didn't think it was an albie, maybe a striper. We were surprised when we finally saw the fish. "Holy shit Phil, it's a bluefish and a big one!"

I knew that fish was going to knock me into second place but if it was going to happen, I was glad it was a close friend who did it. We took some quick photos and he ran off to the Derby Headquarters to weigh it in. It weighed 12.73 lbs.

The fish won a daily gold pin in addition to a Mystery Prize and hung in for the weekly award, and considering the fact that my eleven pound fish held on for two weeks, we were a little more optimistic about its chances for the Grand Prize.

A couple of days later Phil left for home as the All Tackle Shore Bluefish Grand leader but the following week I was throwing eels on the North Shore and caught a 13.33 lb. bluefish and regained the lead. It was one of the biggest Derby bluefish I had ever weighed and after regaining the lead like that, I was starting to think that maybe it was finally in the cards for me.

I didn't have the heart to call Phil but knew he was following the results on line, most likely checking it after every weigh in, and probably every few minutes. He soon called to congratulate me, then had a few unflattering things to say. I think he referred to me as the son of a bad woman. I told him he was not allowed back on the Island until after the Derby.

But it was not meant to be. A couple of days later I got knocked into second place and a few days after that to third, which is where I stayed until 9:30 PM on the last night of the Derby, when I got knocked completely off the leader board.

The fish was still big enough to win the Senior Division and it won the James P. Catlow Memorial Award for the largest shore bluefish caught by a male Island resident. I also scored seven pins and won the Top Rod award for the third time but it stung to get knocked clean off the overall leader board, especially with only thirty minutes left in the five week event. But that's the Derby and the "*thrill of victory.... and the agony of defeat!*"

Finally, if I've had any real measure of success in the thirty years I've been fishing the Derby; it's been in the number of daily pins I've won. To some, winning daily pins means nothing and some even look down on the practice. I don't see it that way.

During the 2013 Derby, Vineyard Gazette reporter Ivy Ashe wrote a piece about daily pins and quoted long time Derby Headquarters administrator and Hall of Fame member Martha Smith as saying, "a pin is better than money. These pins mean so much at all age levels, in all species."

Ivy also spoke with the current Derby Headquarters administrator, Amy Coffey. Amy has worked for the US Olympic Committee and NBC Sports at six different Olympic Games where athletes and spectators trade pins. "The Derby is more pin crazy than that," she says. "They have mass appeal, and unlike Olympic pins, these are more than souvenirs. Derby pins are trophies."

Before I moved to the Island in 2002, I was a competitive master's rower for more than twenty years. As a crew, we put in hundreds of hours and rowed thousands of miles training for a few four minute events every year. One year we won a gold medal at the Masters National Championship and it's hard for me to describe the feelings of pride and accomplishment I got when they placed that gold medal around my neck after the race. After all the miles we rowed and the hours we practiced, it was extremely gratifying to win that event. That medal is very special to me and I feel the same way about my Derby pins. I put a lot of hours and a lot of work into the Derby and to win an award, even something seemingly as small and insignificant as a pin, gives me a sense of accomplishment.

More than 3,000 anglers enter the Derby and like every entrant each time I go fishing I go with the hope of catching a Grand Leader and trying my key in the lock at the awards ceremony. But if all I win is a daily pin, then I'm a happy man. Within the overall five week framework of the Derby there are a series of thirty five daily contests. If I win a daily award, to me it means that out of a hundred or more anglers fishing that day, I was one of the best. It's a feeling that doesn't get old!

EPILOGUE-THIRTY FIRST DERBY

I just completed my thirty first Derby. Not a great Derby for me and painful at times, but looking back on it and in relation to some of the stories I've heard, I think did OK. I weighed in four striped bass, four bluefish, and two false albacore. I won five pins and the Howie Leonard Memorial Award for the largest false albacore caught by a senior. I fished all thirty five days of the event and logged in six to seven hours a day.

As usual, I spent a lot of time prowling the beaches at night and in five weeks saw more beautiful sunrises and sunsets and more shooting stars than most people will see in a lifetime. I fished through two full moons that were so bright you could tie a knot with the light and nights so black you could barely see the tip of your rod. And there were a few magical nights that only a surfcaster could relate to. When you know you are alone on miles of beach surrounded by countless stars and an endless sea, and feel like you are the only person on the planet.

I caught a lot of fish, just not the right one. My "A Spot" from last year produced consistently again but the fish were smaller and although I never ran into anyone else, there were signs my 'secret' spot had been discovered.

I made a couple of new friends and got to know a few others a little better. I did a lot of things right but not everything went my way.

On the last day of the Derby, I forgot to set the free spool lever on my Shimano Baitrunner and wasn't paying attention to the rod in the sand spike. It not only cost me a decent fish, I almost lost a rod and reel.

I was into a school of bonito for three consecutive days and catching one would have eased a lot of pain, but I could not get one to bite and that only added more pain.

Like the song goes, "I did my best but I guess my best wasn't good enough."

I enjoyed seeing my friends catch fish and was thrilled for Ralph Peckham when he caught a 15.18 lb. bluefish that was a Grand Leader. Ralph spends many hours on the beach dunking bait and the Sunday he caught his fish was at his spot for more than ten hours. While the rest of us went home to watch the Patriots beat the Saints, Ralph hung in there and caught his fish shortly after 7:00 PM. If anyone deserved to catch that fish, it was Ralph Peckham. He earned every ounce of it.

Like many Derby anglers, my friends Bob and Fran Clay have an affinity for bonito and false albacore. The Clays live on Chappaquiddick and most of their fishing is done on the Chappy beaches, but they also own a yellow-hulled 30' Contender with twin 300 Yamahas that they moor in Pocha Pond. The boat is named Bonita, which in Spanish and Portuguese translates into 'beautiful'. Their last Contender was named Bonehead for Bob's admitted propensity to run right up to, and sometimes into, breaking fish. A large bonito was painted on the hull of both boats.

Bob was dealing with some health issues this year and didn't fish all that hard, but with three days left in the Derby I was fishing in front of the Windmill House when I saw them motor out of the Gut headed in my direction. They stopped to fish in front of me for a few minutes and then gunned it toward the east and out of sight but less than a half hour later they came flying by in the opposite direction headed toward Edgartown. It was a flat calm morning and they had to be doing close to forty knots.

As a rule the Clays don't weigh fish unless they have a chance at a major prize so it was obvious they were headed to the weigh-in with a big one. I waited about a half hour before I texted them and asked, "OK, how big was it, what kind, and who caught it?" It took a while but eventually a reply came back. "Bob did - a bonito - 11.49 lbs."

The fish was the second largest Derby bonito ever recorded and Bob was one of the four Boat Division Grand Leaders, with a chance to win the Chevy Silverado the Clay Family donates every year. If he was lucky enough to win it he was going to donate it to a local charity. It was Bob's second trip to the awards stage as a Grand Leader. In 2001 he also caught the largest Boat Division Bonito.

To put icing on the cake, Bob and Fran were inducted as a couple into the Derby Hall of Fame

My eighty-two year old co-worker at Larry's, Don MacGilivary, showed he still had the magic by placing third in the All Tackle Boat Bonito Division with a 10.78 lb. fish that was the Grand Leader for one day until Bob caught his. Don holds the Derby record for false albacore and has twice been a Grand Leader.

Jena Lynn Beauregard was the Shore Striped Bass Grand Leader and won the beautiful center console donated by the Eastern Boat Company. Jena is the girlfriend of my friend and co-worker at Larry's, Julian Pepper. Julian is arguably one of the best surfcasters on the Island and in 2012 was a Grand Leader for catching the largest shore bonito. He also won the Shore Grand Slam and placed third in the All Tackle Shore False Albacore Division.

Jena and Julian had put in a few late nights dunking bunker chunks at the proverbial undisclosed location and on the night she caught her fish was so tired she needed to grab some sleep in their car.

Julian stayed at the surf's edge and started to catch fish. He texted Jena and received no response but got her attention when he came back to the car to put a fish in the cooler. Jena groggily dragged herself back to the beach and wasn't there more than ten minutes before Julian slid a 27 lb. fish onto the sand. When another rod went down Julian told her to grab it and she reeled in her 34 lb. winner. The next day at Larry's she had mixed emotions and said she hoped Julian could beat her as it should have been his fish.

Her unabashed show of genuine emotion brought tears of joy to many in attendance at the Awards Ceremony at the Farm Neck Golf Club when her key number eight opened the lock that won the Grand Prize.

In another ceremony the night before, Jena was inducted into the Wentworth Institute of Technology Sports Hall of Fame for her stellar performances as a pitcher on the school softball team. She was described as: "perhaps the greatest pitcher the Wentworth women's softball program has ever seen."

The Derby ended on a great note and in his wrap-up for the Martha's Vineyard Times, Nelson Sigelman's headline stated the event ended "with rousing cheers for a new generation." That was true! In all my years of Derby watching, I never saw two more enthusiastic and genuinely sincere Grand Prize winners than Sam Bell and Jena Beauregard.

Anglers like Sam, Jena and Julian, and Emma and Chase Toomey are great examples of the new generations of Derby fishermen and we will no doubt be seeing their names often on future leader boards. But what really struck me was that anglers like Cooper Gilkes, Ed and Steve Amaral, Bob and Fran Clay, and the "old sailor" Don MacGillivary, who in their sixties, seventies and in Don's case eighties, still have the Derby spirit.

During this year's Derby there were times when it was tough to drag myself out of bed in the middle of the night to fish a tide that for the previous two or three nights had been unproductive. But there were other times when I thought about Coop and the Amarals, who were born and raised here and have fished the Derby since they were young boys, yet still have the enthusiasm and competitive spirit to want to be on the beach dunking bait at four in the morning.

Cooper Gilkes at age sixty-seven was a Grand Leader with a shore bonito and the only angler to record a Shore Grand Slam.

Seventy- six year old Steve Amaral has fished in 67 out of 68 Derby's. Steve fished every night and won the Shore Top Rod Award with a double Hat Trick and eight pins. He also swept the Senior Shore Bass and Bluefish Divisions.

Steve's older brother Ed scored a boat Grand Slam and said he gets so excited after a good night on the beach and a Derby weigh-in he is unable to sleep.

These people are what the Derby is all about!

In thirty-plus years of fishing this great event I've never been a Grand Leader and been close only once, and at my age I know I've slowed a little and lost just a bit of my competitive edge. But as long as there is a truck, boat, plaque, or even a pin up for grabs, and as long as the good Lord wills it, I'll be back next year and every year I'm physically able.

"Many think it's about the fish. It's really about the people. Go to the Derby headquarters, the tackle shops or the beaches, and you see the Derby spirit." Derby Chairman, John Custer.

GLOSSARY OF TERMS

Weigh-in: Also known as Derby Headquarters. The place where Derby entrants weigh their fish. During the Derby the weigh-in is open from 8:00-10:00 AM and 8:00-10:00 PM every day.

The 'Board' or Leader Board: The Leader Boards are located at Derby Headquarters. There are numerous boards, including the Grand Leader Board which is located behind the official Derby weigh scale, but also Daily, Weekly, Team, Senior, Junior, Flyrod, and Grand Slam. The Boards at Derby Headquarters are updated by hand after each weigh-in period. At the close of every day, computer printed results are also posted outside Derby Headquarters and 'real-time' information is available on the Derby web-site .

Making the Board: Catching a fish that is big enough to get your name on the 'Board.'

Grand Leader: At the end of the Derby an entrant who has caught the largest of one of the four eligible species from the Boat or Shore Divisions. There are eight Grand Leaders, four from each division.

Key: At the Derby Awards Ceremony held the Sunday after the tournament ends the eight Grand Leaders are given a key. Each key is tried in a lock and the angler holding the key that opens the lock is awarded the Grand Prize for that division. Shore Division key holders have a chance to win a fully equipped boat, motor and trailer and Boat Division key holders an opportunity to win a full size truck.

Pin: Gold (1st), Silver (2nd), Bronze(3rd) and Pewter (4th) pins are awarded on a daily basis for each species, division and category excluding False Albacore. During the course of the Derby anglers may win only one first, one second, one third, and one fourth daily pin, for each species, category and division. If an angler qualifies for a prize he/she has already won, they are awarded the next highest prize for which they are eligible. (Depending upon their daily award, winners also receive a small cash prize ranging from $20 to $5.)

Hat Trick: A special pin awarded to the angler, boat and shore, who win a first, second, third, and fourth Daily Prize in a species category. Anglers can win only one Hat Trick per species.

Mystery Prize: A luck of the draw prize usually consisting of approximately $100 worth of fishing tackle. One mystery prize, per species excluding False Albacore, is awarded daily. The winner is drawn from all fish weighed in, boat and shore.

Weekly: During the course of the Derby weekly prizes are presented to the anglers catching the largest fish of each species, in each category and division, including False Albacore. The weekly prize includes a special pin as well as fishing tackle.

Grand Slam: A separate category within the overall framework of the Derby. Awards are given to the 1st, 2nd and 3rd place anglers in the All Tackle and Flyrod Divisions, Boat and Shore, who weigh in the heaviest aggregate weight of all four eligible Derby species. An angler who achieves a Grand Slam is awarded a special pin regardless of their overall finish.

Top Rod: A special prize awarded to the entrant who wins the highest number of Daily Pins in the All Tackle Division at the close of the Derby. There are separate awards for the Shore, Boat and Junior categories.

ACKNOWLEDGEMENTS

'Three Decades of The Derby' was an easy book to write because of my affection for the Derby and the people I've met and fished with over the years. In the process I received a lot of satisfaction from friends who commented about bringing back memories of the good old days.

Most of the stories in the book came from thirty years of fishing logs and a fading memory, but I had a lot of help from the anglers themselves or their families and friends. I am grateful to Dan Williams and Maryann Henninger for their help with the chapter on Abe. Thanks to Mary Ann, Anthony and Peter Angelone. I know it wasn't easy. Michael Ditchfield added some great color by providing me with an amusing story about his Dad - thank you Michael.

Mark Carlson sent along some photos that helped me remember just how good it was - thanks Mark.

Nelson Sigelman, Editor of the Martha's Vineyard Times did the background research on Al Angelone and gave me permission to use it - thank you Nelson.

Thanks to Keith McArt, the other half of Team McRat, as well as Bob 'Hawkeye' Jacobs and Ron McKee -Team Rusty Hooks.

Paul Schultz, Chip Bergeron, Paula Sullivan, John Schillinger, Pat Abate, Bob McKay, Julian Pepper, Mark Wrabel, Chuck and Ebba

Hodgkinson, Dave and Robin Nash, Dave Balon, Lance and Lois Dimock, Ed Amaral, Jim and Debbie Hendrickson, Tony and Chrissy Maio, Joe Gubitose, Bob and Fran Clay, Roger and Tracy Ardanowski, Phil and Sharon Cronin, Tom Kieras. Walter Lison, and Sue Quirk all contributed, thank you.

While I was writing the book I had serious doubts about whether readers beyond my family and friends would like it. In an attempt to ease my fears I ran a few chapters past my friends Pat Blasi, Phil Henning, Mark Carlson, and my daughters Kari and Chrissy and they encouraged me to continue. When I finally finished, my friend and fellow surfcaster Paul Apuzzo read the entire manuscript and boosted my confidence by assuring me it was good enough to publish and that anglers, especially surf fishermen, would enjoy it. I am grateful to all of you for your positive feedback and support.

Dave Kinney is a Pulitzer Prize winning journalist and author of the great book about the 2007 Derby, 'The Big One.' His latest book 'The Dylanologists' is a look at Bob Dylan through the eyes of his fans and followers. Dave picked me up when I was at my lowest point when he said he *'liked it'* and they were good stories. He also provided valuable input regarding content and copy. Thanks Dave!

Last, but by no means least, thank you Barbara for being the person you are. Thanks also for your inspiration as well as putting up with years of listening to my Derby tales of woe. Finally, thank you for changing all those exclamation points to periods and remembering your high school grammar lessons.

Made in the USA
Lexington, KY
10 September 2016